FOR JOLEEN AND CALEB

Copyright 2015 by Emerge Creatives Group LLP and Daniel Ling.
All rights reserved. Printed in Singapore. No part of this publication may be reproduced, stored in a retrieval system, or transmitted, in any form or by any means, electronic, mechanical, photocopying, recording or otherwise, without the permission of the publisher.

For design thinking training workshops, talks or consultation with expert design thinker Daniel Ling, contact emerge.creatives@gmail.com to discuss opportunities.

FOREWORD
BY DANIEL LING

Design must reflect the practical and aesthetic in business but above all...
good design must primarily serve people.
- Thomas J Watson, Industrialist

In Apple's early days, Mike Markkula, one of its first investors, wrote a one-page memo dubbed "The Apple Marketing Philosophy".

In particular, three points were stressed:
• **Empathy** - an intimate understanding of the customer. Markkula set down this marker to the rest of his team: "We will truly understand their needs better than any other company."

• **Focus** - a defined and unwavering action plan. "In order to do a good job of those things that we decide to do, we must eliminate all of the unimportant opportunities," said Markkula.

• **Impute** - belief that people will subconsciously judge a company, based on the product, its packaging and service by its staff. "People DO judge a book by its cover," he wrote. "We may have the best product, the highest quality, the most useful software- if we present them in a slipshod manner, they will be perceived as slipshod; it we present them in a creative, professional manner, we will impute the desired qualities."

This memo, written in the early 1980s before the MacIntosh launch, was insightful. These values really articulate what sets Apple apart from its rivals. Today, we can see that a lot of work goes into the product design and user interface design of an iPhone or a Macbook. Thought and focus goes into the way into its packaging, even the way the phone is taken out of the box. Deep empathy of customers is required to deliver a pleasant customer experience of purchasing music from iTunes.

Although he didn't realize it at that time, Markkula was writing about some of the fundamentals of design thinking.

ACKNOWLEDGEMENTS
BY DANIEL LING

I am a firm believer that everyone can be a designer- that we need more designers in a business suit.

I have close to 10 years of experience in innovation and design thinking in the area of the product and service design industry- who has moulded myself to be a "designer in a business suit"- strong in the design thinking process but yet relevant to business and financial industry. My years of experience in facilitation in workshops and training will bring practical knowledge to real life context.

I am driven by a vision to empower professionals and students with design thinking skills to be able to bring innovation and personal effectiveness to solve problems for the organization. And I do hope that by creating a book like this- I could share my knowledge as a design thinker to a larger audience, passionate about what they do and knowing that they too, can make a change in business or society.

I wish to personally thank the following people for their contributions to my inspiration and knowledge and other help in creating this book:

My wife Joleen and my son Caleb
- For being patient and gracious in allowing me to give up some precious quality time with you, to spend writing this book. It wasn't easy.

My mentor and boss Bojan
- For moulding and giving me opportunities to be moulded as one of the design and user experience experts in the industry.

Colleagues Mingjie and Jordan
- For inspiring me to start writing this book. The inertia was great but I bucked it down after that inspiring coffee chat.

Illustrator Stefanie and Copywriter Han Hwee
- Thanks for the support in making this book happen!

CONTENTS

Chapter 1
What's Design Thinking   **9**

Why do we need design thinking?
What makes design thinking unique?
Design thinking checklist

Chapter 2
Design Action Plan   **27**

5 characteristics of action plan
Empathize phase
       - User feedback template
       - Personas template
       - Empathy map template
Define phase
       - Design brief template
       - Stakeholder map template
       - Customer journey template
       - Context map template
       - Opportunity map template
Ideate phase
       - Prioritistation map template
       - Affinity map template
       - Evaluate ideas template
Prototype phase
       - Physical prototype example
       - Wireframe example
       - Storyboard template
Test phase
       - User feedback template
       - Prototype evaluation template

Chapter 3
5 Thinking Mindsets   **67**

Summary of 5 mindsets
Anatomy of a design thinker
Mindset 1: Think users first
Mindset 2: Ask the right questions
Mindset 3; Believe you can draw
Mindset 4: Commit to ideate
Mindset 5: Prototype to test

Chapter 4
Think Users First   **85**

What are your users inherent needs?
How do you empathize your users?
Ask questions- What you need to know
Steps to take for preparing an interview
Persona
Empathy map

Chapter 5
Ask The Right Questions   **101**

Why ask the right questions?
What are different type of questions?
Who should you ask questions?
How to align stakeholders in meetings?
Design brief
Stakeholder map
Customer journey
Context map
Opportunity map

Chapter 6
Believe You Can Draw **123**

Why should we communicate by drawing?
What is the value of drawing?
How to start drawing?
    - Visual library
    - Journey or process
    - Problem
    - Communication
How to start facilitation by drawing?

Chapter 7
Commit To Ideate **141**

Why do you need to ideate?
What are the rules of ideation?
How to facilitate an ideation session?
How to build a creative culture?
Divergent- 5 common ideation techniques
    - Brainwriting
    - Nyaka method
    - NHK method
    - Scamper
    - What if?
Convergent- 3 simple ways to converge
    - Prioritisation map
    - Affinity map
    - Idea evaluation

Chapter 8
Prototype To Test **167**

What you could use as a prototype?
Why do we need a prototype?
Why do we test?
How to conduct a structured test?
How to conduct the interview?
How to conduct the observers' debrief?

"DESIGN'S FUNDAMENTAL ROLE IS PROBLEM SOLVER."

- FAST COMPANY, BUSINESS MAGAZINE

CHAPTER 1

WHAT'S DESIGN THINKING?

CHAPTER 1
WHAT'S DESIGN THINKING?

So what is design thinking, and how can this help us?

Design thinking is part and parcel of what goes through a designer's mind in every single design project. It is a powerful thinking tool that can drive a brand, business or an individual forward positively.

An example would be to take a gadget and ask, "How do I make this work, better, faster, smoother, and reduce waste and inefficiency?" But it can go beyond product design. You can scale it up and apply it to many things. For example, as more and more people come to cities to look for jobs, these urban areas' consumption of energy, food, water, and other natural resources will steadily increase.

This naturally places great pressure and stress not just on our environments, but on our daily living and routines (this goes a long way to explain Singapore's traffic jams, long queues, and overcrowded malls).

Design thinking can help solve problems with overcrowded living spaces, and minimize stress to our infrastructure. It can be used to utilize our resources effectively, and minimize energy consumption.

However, this book is not trying to sell design thinking to 'replace' your existing thinking techniques - but rather as a 'complement' or 'add-on'. Some people will wonder - what is so great about thinking like a designer? Firstly, it is a tried and trusted problem-solving thinking tool that anyone can employ to achieve real, concrete results. However, if you did not use it consistently enough, and actively integrate it in your mindset, you may not be able to see effective results.

However, the real question to ask is, "Why not?" Isn't it good to have another set of tools to help you excel?

CHAPTER 1 — WHAT'S DESIGN THINKING?

WHY DO WE NEED DESIGN THINKING?

3 key factors why people need design thinking:

For companies to innovate

"Innovation distinguishes between a leader and a follower."
- Steve Jobs, Apple CEO

Companies need to innovate or die. Today's consumers are very aware, are spoiled for choice, and can be very fickle.

3M and Apple were companies on the brink of failure- but they proceed to adopt an innovative culture through design thinking to achieve amazing records of success. Today, 3M generated nearly $30 billion revenue selling over 55,000 innovative products, while Apple captivated the consumer electronics market with stylish products like the iPhone, Macbook and iPad.

In a competitive market, companies, big or small, need to innovate to create an advantage over their competitors. Design thinking will allow companies and startups to innovate and explore opportunities, based on unmet consumer needs and understanding of the situation.

Apple adopted an innovative culture through design thinking to achieve an amazing record of success.

CHAPTER 1 — WHAT'S DESIGN THINKING?

WHY DO WE NEED DESIGN THINKING?

3 key factors why people need design thinking:

For society
to solve human problems

"Design is directed toward human beings. To design is to solve human problems by identifying them and executing the best solution."
- Ivan Chermayeff, Designer & Artist

People need design thinking to solve human problems (difficulties we encounter in daily life). For example, we face issues like overcrowding at train stations, bad online banking experiences and traffic jams, which can lead to frustration and social problems. By applying design thinking principles, we identify the best possible options to streamline and make these experiences go better, faster and smoother.

Overcrowding on Singapore's MRT - can we solve it?

13

WHY DO WE NEED DESIGN THINKING?

3 key factors why people need design thinking:

For individuals to compete

"Design thinking is a human-centered approach to innovation that draws from the designer's toolkit to integrate the needs of people, the possibilities of technology, and the requirements for business success."
- Tim Brown, President & CEO of IDEO

Design thinking has already been seen as a competitive advantage for individuals who want to excel in their career or business. Many schools, such as the Rotman School of Design and Stanford University's d.school, have offered exclusive courses on Design Thinking to executives and professionals. They aim to give students with design backgrounds a stronger business advantage, while offering business-minded people a more creative edge.

According to the Wall Street Journal, prospects are willing to pay up to $40,000 per year for a Design Thinking MBA, while a Stanford's three-day Design Thinking bootcamp costs $9,500!

There are many individuals willing to fork out huge money to gain valuable design thinking tools and knowledge - all in order to compete, and be more effective.

Prospects are willing to fork out huge money to gain an advantage valuable design thinking tools and knowledge - all in order to compete and be more effective.

CHAPTER 1 — WHAT'S DESIGN THINKING?

Thinking like a designer can transform the way organizations develop products and services on the front end. It can also improve processes and strategy in the backend. You can apply the principles to a new product or service, but you can also use to tackle a problem that a plagues a city or nation.

It is a way to think and ideate on a solution to address a problem, or better meet a customer need. It is a process focused on solutions, and not on problems.

ACTIVITY

After understanding why we need design thinking, here are some follow-up reflections.

What are the **key innovations** that inspire you?
How could you make some things better?

What are some **human problems** that you face everyday?
How would you solve them?

What will design thinking help you to **compete** in?

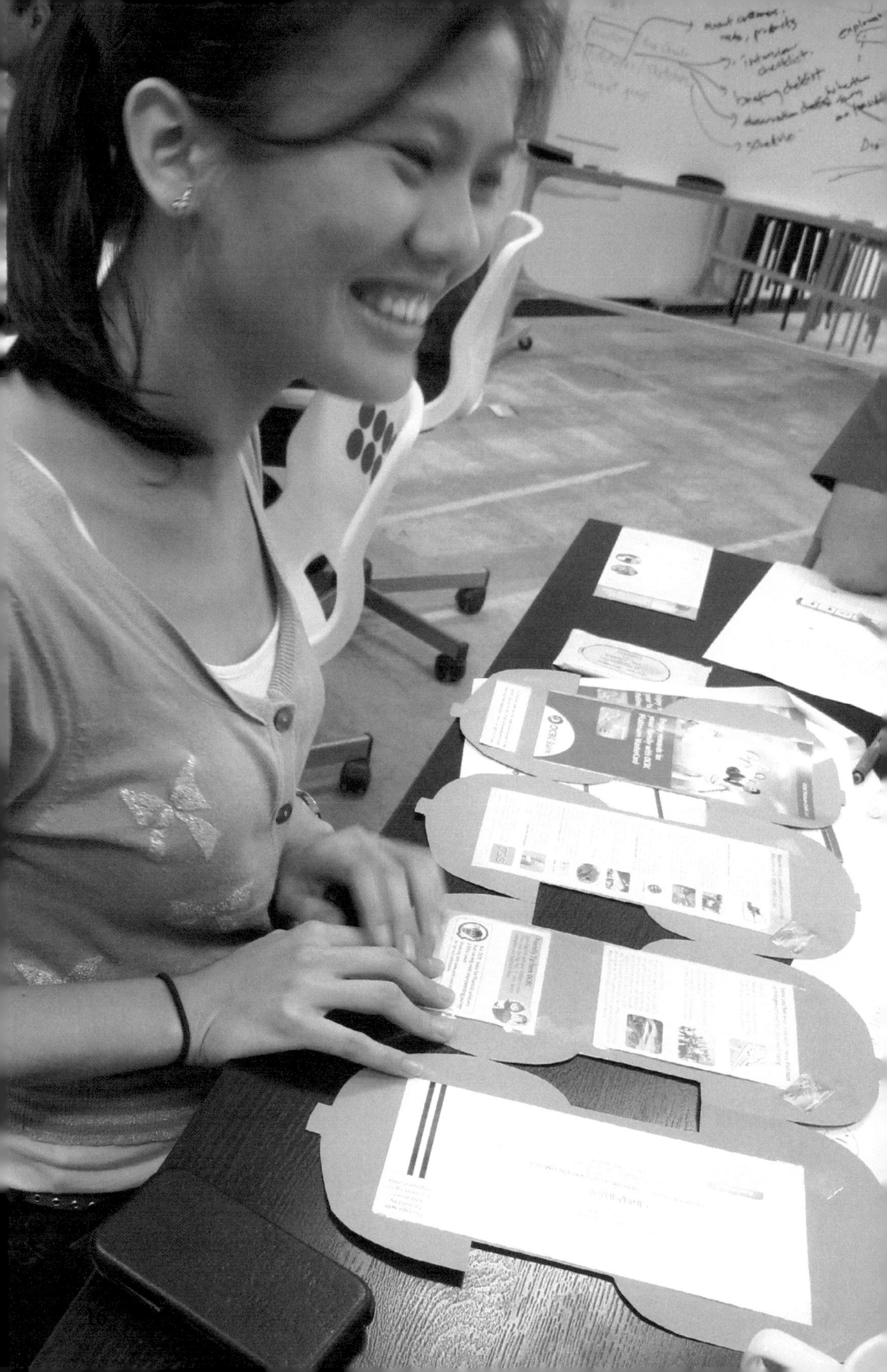

WHAT MAKES DESIGN THINKING A UNIQUE WAY OF THINKING?
7 characteristics that define design thinking

In psychology, it is believed that the left brain controls the more logical, analytical functions, whereas the right hemisphere processes the imagination, creativity and emotions.

Design thinking is probably one of the few disciplines that utilize both equally. However, it is not a genetic gift that only a few people possess. Just remember:

Anyone can use design thinking.

It is **fun.**

It involves methods that enable **empathy with people.**

It seeks to **define the problem** as actively as finding the solution.

It **ideates and explores solutions.**

It is **collaborative** and involves **iterative prototyping.**

It solves problems of **many different types.**

CHAPTER 1 — WHAT'S DESIGN THINKING?

ACTIVITY

Can you think of problems that occur in:

Society

- Overcrowding on buses
- Young couples unable to afford houses
-
-
-

Business & Services

- Bad online experience buying movie tickets
-
-
-

Process & Operations

- Backlog issues
- Unable to tackle an issue efficiently
-
-
-

Situations

- When haze arrives
- When customer complains
-
-
-

WHAT MAKES DESIGN THINKING A UNIQUE WAY OF THINKING?

How is design thinking compared to other ways of thinking:

Business Thinking	**Design Thinking**	Creative Thinking
Left brain	**Using both sides of the brain to solve problems**	Right brain
Rational and structured	**Switching at will between rational and intuitive approach**	Intuitive and emotional
Focus on analysis	**Iterating between analysis and creation**	Focus on creation / expression
Deal with well-defined problems	**Deal with ill-defined problems**	Deal with no or undefined problems
Target to improve business results	**Target to improve user's experience**	Target to explore new ideas
Analyze > Decide	**Empathize > Define > Ideate > Prototype > Test**	Perceive > Ideate
"Let's solve this problem."	**"What is the problem we are trying to solve?"**	"There is no problem!"

"DESIGN IS SO CRITICAL IT SHOULD BE ON THE AGENDA OF EVERY MEETING IN EVERY SINGLE DEPARTMENT."

- TOM PETERS, AUTHOR ON BUSINESS MANAGEMENT

DESIGN THINKING - ACTION PLAN WITH 5 THINKING MINDSETS
Understand the framework of design thinking:

If we break it down into its components, design thinking is made of two distinct root words - "design" and "think".

"Design" is derived from "Dēsignāre" in Latin which means "to mark out and take action", while **"Think"** comes from "Cogito" which means "to ponder and consider".

Hence, design thinking is the proper attitude and frame of mind, along with the right series of actions, in order to solve a problem. If the mindset is the train, then the action plan is the track.

design + thinking

Action Plan   Mindsets

In any venture, you need some form of strategy or battle plan.

A **design action plan** is a series of action phases that execute the design thinking process. We will go into greater detail about the characteristics of a design plan in chapter 2.

A **mindset** a set of thinking traits or behaviors that runs the design thinking process consistently and effectively. This will be developed and expanded upon in chapter 3.

YOU NEED THE ACTION PLAN AND THE MINDSETS TO RUN TOGETHER!

You need both the action plan and mindset in order to run design thinking. One will not work without the other.

To use an analogy, imagine a car and a driver. The car will not move without the driver turning on the ignition, and the driver cannot travel without a car. Similarly, effective design thinking requires both the design action plan (the car) and the mindset (the driver) to function together properly.

This is critically important. If the user does not have the correct mindset to begin with, he/she is likely to become frustrated, and waste a lot of time and effort. Even the best action plans are likely to go wrong, under such circumstances.

DESIGN THINKING CHECKLIST -
WHAT TOOLS AND RESOURCES DO YOU NEED?

Ensure you have the design thinking tools and resources:

- Good collaborative space

- Paper

- Writing tools

- Cutting and sticking tools

- Camera / Images

- Sketchbook

- Post-its

- Cardboard

- Whiteboard / Wall / Pin board

- Cards

- Materials for prototyping

- Frameworks (which you will learn from this book)

DESIGN THINKING CHECKLIST – DO YOU HAVE WHAT IT TAKES TO BE A DESIGN THINKER?

Find out whether you have the traits of a design thinker:

Step into the shoes of your customers

Have empathy on users and stakeholders

Like to challenge the status quo rebelliously

Able to ask the right questions- even to your boss

Draw and sketch instead of typing an email

Like to collaborate in multi-disciplinary meetings instead of working in silo

Look at the big picture and think holistically

Generate many new ideas and not afraid to share

Find and reiterate alternatives to approach your desired goals

Willing to fail early and often

This is a self-assessment and not a test!
Remember, anyone can be a design thinker!

If you score 8-10/10, great! Keep it up! Your mindsets are strong to be a design thinker, and you will find your traits to appear often through the course of this book.

If you score 4-7/10, you are on your way! Most of you should be in this category. Continue to hone and master your design thinking traits through the course of this book.

If you score 0-3/10, its ok! That's why you are working on it and reading this book. Having the mindsets and traits of a design thinker is definitely achievable.

SUMMARY POINTS

People need design thinking:
- To innovate
- To solve human problems
- To compete

Design thinking is really about having a design action plan with a set of thinking mindsets.

Do you have the tools and resources?

Do you have the traits to be a design thinker?

"DESIGN IS NOT JUST WHAT IT LOOKS AND FEELS LIKE. DESIGN IS HOW IT WORKS."

—STEVE JOBS, APPLE CEO

CHAPTER 2
DESIGN ACTION PLAN

CHAPTER 2
DESIGN ACTION PLAN

As stated earlier in chapter 1, you do not plunge into design thinking, with no idea, and no strategy. You need a design action plan.

The design action plan is a framework that contains a series of action phases that execute the design thinking process. It is a roadmap that tells people involved in a project whether they are going to be on the right track.

The 5 action phases are:

Empathize - to understand your customers / users
Define - to define clear project / business objectives
Ideate - to explore ideas and solutions
Prototype - to build and visualise ideas and solutions
Test - to review and decide

5 CHARACTERISTICS OF ACTION PLAN

It is **not just a brainstorming session** or a "one-day" process.

The design action plan is not a process that works instantaneously - it requires time and effort from committed individuals involved with the same objective to make it work. It is certainly not a "one-day" process where problems can be solved in 24 hours. There are phases where you need multiple iterations, testing and checking back with users and exploration where it would take time to incubate.

Some have commercialized design thinking as a "brainstorming" session. It is not. Remember, design thinking is a 5-step process, and not a 1-step *Ideate Phase*. It seeks to define the problem, even as it finds the solution.

It is a **iterative** process.

The design action plan is an iterative process. You need to repeat each phase backwards and forwards, and arrives at each decision or desired result, after rounds of discovery. It means to work on something over and over again, until every facet becomes crystal clear.

For example, you can iterate between *Ideate and Prototype Phase* several times - you sketch ideas and immediately build prototypes to make rounds and rounds of discovery of the idea. After that, you may want to go back to Ideate Phase to refine the ideas yet again.

YOU NEED TO REPEAT EACH PHASE BACKWARDS AND FORWARDS, AND ARRIVES AT EACH DECISION OR DESIRED RESULT, AFTER ROUNDS OF DISCOVERY.
IT MEANS TO WORK ON SOMETHING OVER AND OVER AGAIN, UNTIL EVERY FACET BECOMES CRYSTAL CLEAR.

— THE ITERATIVE PROCESS

5 CHARACTERISTICS OF ACTION PLAN

It contains phases of both **divergent** and **convergent** thinking.

The design action plan has phases of both divergent and convergent thinking.

The *Empathise and Ideate Phase* requires divergent thinking. Divergent thinking is to create and explore ideas and possibilities, without restraint. Within the phase, you will be encouraged to make guesses, come out with wild ideas and be creative.

The *Define, Prototype and Test Phase* requires convergent thinking. Convergent thinking means to actively select and decide the right solutions to the problem, based on constraints or feedback. Within the phase, you will be encouraged to analyze and make decisions and constantly ask critical questions to solve the problems at hand.

Both sides of thinking are important in order to make this process work.

5 CHARACTERISTICS OF ACTION PLAN

It requires everyone to **collaborate** and go through the process together.

The design action plan is made up of phases where everyone, including the design thinking facilitator, collaborates on the process together.

Everyone will bring their prior experiences and knowledge about the problem to the table and work on the issue together.

The process is not like a hot potato, where you "toss" the responsibility from one individual to another. For example, the researcher in the *Empathize Phase* might share to the business lead in the *Define Phase* and define the project, which engages a designer to coordinate the *Ideate Phase,* and then leave everything to the engineer in the *Prototype and Test Phase!*

But this is not proper design thinking. Instead, all of them (the researcher, business lead, designer and engineer) should be in the process from start to end.

This is because everyone in the team requires deep insight of what the issues are and what are needs of the user s- so that everybody is on the same page. Design thinking is a process where everyone collaborates together from start till end with a common objective.

Design thinking is a process where everyone collaborates together from start till end with a common objective.

5 CHARACTERISTICS OF ACTION PLAN

There are **deliverables** at every phase.

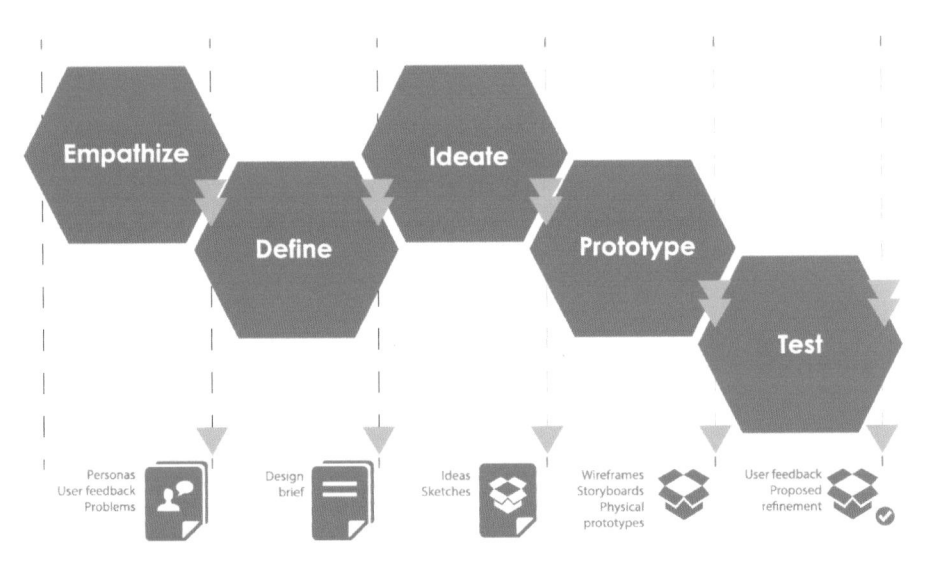

```
Empathize → Define → Ideate → Prototype → Test
```

- Personas, User feedback, Problems
- Design brief
- Ideas, Sketches
- Wireframes, Storyboards, Physical prototypes
- User feedback, Proposed refinement

There is a deliverable outcome of each action phase which will give you a point of reference, when you go through the process of iteration. This list of deliverables is not exhaustive, but you do not have to use them all. Based on the nature of your project, select the necessary deliverable.

At the end of each phase we have:

1. Empathize Phase:
Personas
Empathy map
List of user feedback
Problems identified

3. Ideate Phase:
Ideas / concepts
Sketches
Prioritisation map
Affinity map
Idea evaluation

5. Test Phase:
List of user feedback
Observation
Evaluation map
Proposed refinement

2. Define Phase:
Design brief
Stakeholder map
Context map
Customer journeys
Opportunity map

4. Prototype Phase:
Physical prototypes
Wireframes
Storyboards

5 CHARACTERISTICS OF ACTION PLAN - SUMMARY

Characteristics	What would you expect	What is expected of you?
1. Not just a brainstorming session	Proactive process of action phases over a period of time	Be patient and prepared that the process does not work like instantaneously
2. Iterative process	Repeated rounds of discovery of ideas / concepts until you become crystal clear	Be willing to discover and never stop at the first idea / concept
3. Has phases of both divergent and convergent thinking	Explore ideas & possibilities at one action phase while being decisive in solutions in another	Approach different way of thinking at each action phase
4. Requires collaboration	All stakeholders go through the process together	Be open and accept others into the process- everyone has experience and expertise to bring to the table
5. Deliverables at every phase	Point of reference at every action phase	Advocate to document deliverables at every phase

ACTIVITY
Think you are ready to design?

Design your ideal Wearable Technology.

5 PHASES OF THE ACTION PLAN

There are 5 phases of the action plan - each phase has its own objective, activities, tools and deliverables. For the rest of this chapter, I will expand and elaborate on these 5 phases, so that you will be clear of what each one requires.

Empathize - to understand your customers / users
Define - to define clear project / business objectives
Ideate - to explore ideas and solutions
Prototype - to build and visualise ideas and solutions
Test - to review and decide

Next, we will do an exercise and design a piece of Wearable Technology. I have included a design action plan framework, complete with a set of instructions, tools and basic deliverable templates to help you kick off your design thinking journey.

Make sure that you try out each quick activity at each phase. This will give you an idea of what it takes and what it is required of you to go through each phase. Try and stick to the suggested timings, so you don't overrun.

SUMMARY OF THE 5 ACTION PHASES

Phase:	Activities:	Tools to use:	Deliverables:
1. Empathise	User interview Informal chats Observation Shadowing Mystery shopping Picture-taking Immersion	Interview checklist Observation checklist Writing tools Flipcharts and paper Camera	Personas Empathy Map List of user feedback Problems identified
2. Define	Workshops Stakeholder meetings	Drawing and writing tools Post-its Flipchart / Whiteboard User feedback *(from Empathize)*	Design brief Stakeholder map Context map Customer journeys Opportunity map
3. Ideate	Ideation activities Brainstorming workshops Mindmaps Sketching / drawing	Drawing and writing tools Post-its Flipchart / Whiteboard Personaa *(from Empathize)* Design brief *(from Define)* Brainstorming tools	Ideas / concepts Sketches Prioritisation map Affinity map Idea evaluation
4. Prototype	Space prototyping Physical prototyping Paper construction Wireframe building Storyboards Role-plays	Paper Cardboard Construction materials Cutting and writing tools Space Props	Physical prototypes Wireframes Storyboards
5. Test	User testing Observation Picture-taking Evaluation discussion	Briefing checklist Interview checklist Observation checklist Prototypes to test *(from Prototype)*	List of user feedback Observation Evaluation map Proposed refinement

CHAPTER 2 — EMPATHIZE PHASE

1. EMPATHIZE PHASE

Objective:

The *Empathize Phase* is the first phase of the design thinking process. During this phase, you will need to immerse yourself in learning about others, primarily the end users, and the problem that you are trying to solve.

You can also talk to experts and other key stakeholders, or even conduct research and interviews. Your goal is to develop background knowledge through these experiences, and use these insights as a springboard to address design challenges.

Activities:

User interview
Informal chats
Observation
Shadowing
Mystery shopping
Picture-taking
Immersion

Tools to use:

Interview checklist
Observation checklist
Writing tools
Flipcharts and paper
Camera

Deliverables:

Personas
Empathy Map
List of user feedback
Problems identified

CHAPTER 2　　　　　　　　　　　　　　　　　　　　　　　　　　　EMPATHIZE PHASE

QUICK EMPATHIZE ACTIVITY - 14 MINS

You have a new mission- instead of thinking of ideas on your own with Wearable Technology- go through the Empathize Phase to understand your users!

Design a Wearable Technology that is useful and meaningful for your partner.

What questions would you ask your partner? Write it down.

- What do you do and what is your lifestyle? What are gadgets and technology you use?
- What information do you need while you are travelling or moving around?
- Why do you need the information?
- What are the problems you face while traveling or moving around?
- When ...
- Where ...
- Who ...
- How ...

-
-
-
-

Take down notes of your partner's response. Remember to observe, listen and empathize what he/she say.

Build a persona / empathy map!

USER FEEDBACK TEMPLATE
EMPATHISE PHASE DELIVERABLE

Empathize your end-users by writing down what you observe and listen

Customer profile:

Questions to ask:

| List of questions | Why do we ask these questions? |

User feedback:

| Observations and feedback | Insights / Actions |

PERSONAS TEMPLATE
EMPATHISE PHASE DELIVERABLE

Empathize your end-users on who they are

Name:

Profile / Lifestyle:

Characteristics

Goals / Ambitions

Behaviors / Habits

Fears / Challenges

Influencers and Activities

EMPATHY MAP TEMPLATE
EMPATHISE PHASE DELIVERABLE

Empathize your end-users on what they think and feel

Think and Feel

Hear Your customer See

Say and Do

Pain Gain

2. DEFINE PHASE

Objective:

Define is the convergent phase where you make informed decisions from the insights gained from Empathize. You develop clarity by asking the right critical questions to the stakeholders or team members involved in the same project. You get curious and find out things. You challenge the status quo, and might even open up cans of worms (be tactful, or you might make some enemies too :P

Based fully on the insights, you ask these questions:

- What is the problem we are trying to solve?
- Where are we heading?
- Who are we helping?
- What is the value proposition?
- What is our situation?
- How did this happen?

Activities:

Workshops
Stakeholder meetings

Tools to use:

Drawing and writing tools
Post-its
Flipchart / Whiteboard
User feedback
(from Empathize)

Deliverables:

Design brief
Stakeholder map
Context map
Customer journeys
Opportunity map

Stakeholder meetings

QUICK DEFINE ACTIVITY - 14 MINS

Before you present your design brief to the management, you need to spend time to define and explain. Remember, the more clearly you define things, the easier it will be for your management to identify opportunities and problems.

Define the Wearable Technology business case to present to your management.

Insights to my partner's lifestyle and needs

Insights to my partner's problems while travelling / moving around

How do you propose what you should do? Write it down.

I will design for **(target customer)** who has **(customer need)**, **(Wearable Technology name)** has **(one key benefit)** because of **(one key reason)**.

Discuss with you group on any **one of** the stakeholder map / context map / customer journeys / opportunity map.

Build your design brief.

DESIGN BRIEF TEMPLATE
DEFINE PHASE DELIVERABLE
Define the project with your design objective and requirements

User perception / feedback

Problem statement

Design goal / objective

Design requirements

- Our product / service should ....

-
-
-
-

STAKEHOLDER MAP TEMPLATE
DEFINE PHASE DELIVERABLE
Define the project by identifying the roles and relationship of your stakeholders

Vendors / Influencers

External stakeholders

Project team

CUSTOMER JOURNEY TEMPLATE
DEFINE PHASE DELIVERABLE

Define the project by knowing what your customers go through

- Backen Processes
- Emotions
- Thoughts
- Touchpoints
- Customer Actions
- Activity Phase

CONTEXT MAP TEMPLATE
DEFINE PHASE DELIVERABLE

Define the project by understanding the factors surrounding your design intent

Target users / User needs

Technology factors

Business factors

Trends

Uncertainties

Other questions?

Other questions?

Other questions?

49

OPPORTUNITY MAP TEMPLATE
DEFINE PHASE DELIVERABLE
Define the project by identifying the opportunity

Factor X

Design D

Design A

Design C

Design B

Factor Y

Design E

Design H

Area of opportunity

Area of opportunity

Design I

Design G

Design F

3. IDEATE PHASE

Objective:

Ideate Phase is the critical and most celebrated phase of the design thinking process. You will be challenged to think out of the box and to brainstorm a myriad of ideas. You will suspend all kinds of judgment to your ideas and solutions. No idea is too far-fetched and no one's ideas are rejected. Ideating is all about creativity and fun.

Quantity is encouraged. Your team will generate a hundred ideas in a single session. You and your team will be encouraged to be dreamers of the impossible and visionaries of the future.

Activities:

Ideation activities
Brainstorming workshops
Mindmaps
Sketching / drawing

Tools to use:

Drawing and writing tools
Post-its
Flipchart / Whiteboard
Personaa *(from Empathize)*
Design brief *(from Define)*
Brainstorming tools

Deliverables:

Ideas / concepts
Sketches
Prioritisation map
Affinity map
Idea evaluation

Brainstorming on post-its

QUICK IDEATE ACTIVITY - 7 MINS

You will get to learn some ideation techniques in Chapter 7. Have a shot with coming up with ideas of your Wearable Technology now!

Sketch out 5 radical ideas based on your design brief!

Prioritize, categorize or evaluate your ideas using the prioritization map / affinity map / evaluate ideas templates.

PRIORITISATION MAP TEMPLATE
IDEATE PHASE DELIVERABLE

Organise your ideas by prioritising based on benefit and ease of implementation

High Benefit

Idea D

Idea A

Idea C

Easy to Implement

Idea B

Difficult to Implement

Idea E

Idea H

Idea I

Idea F

Idea G

Low Benefit

AFFINITY MAP TEMPLATE
- IDEATE PHASE DELIVERABLE

Organise your ideas by grouping them in broad categories

Random Post-its of ideas

Categorise and group the ideas

EVALUATE IDEAS TEMPLATE
IDEATE PHASE DELIVERABLE

Organise your ideas by evaluating based on a set of criterias

Evaluation Criteria	Customer Impact	Business Impact	Potential Improvement	Feasibility	Innovativeness	XYZ
Idea A	− +	− +	− +	− +	− +	− +
Idea B						
Idea C						
Idea D						

4. PROTOTYPE PHASE

Objective:

Prototyping is a rough and rapid portion of the design thinking process. A prototype can be a paper model, storyboard, wireframe or a cardboard box - it allows you to quickly visualize and identify the best solution among several concepts. It is a way to convey an idea quickly. The fidelity of the prototype does not matter.

You will learn to experiment and that it is better to fail early and often.

Activities:

Space prototyping
Physical prototyping
Paper construction
Wireframe building
Storyboards
Role-plays

Tools to use:

Paper
Cardboard
Construction materials
Cutting and writing tools
Space
Props

Deliverables:

Physical prototypes
Wireframes
Storyboards

Experimenting with shapes

Creating role-plays with cardboards

QUICK PROTOTYPE ACTIVITY - 30 MINS
Here is the fun part. Get your selected concept out visually so that you can get feedback and impression.

Get feedback and prototype your selected idea!

> Prototype your Wearable Technology using anything from scrap paper, straws, cardboards or post-its. Main idea is to bring your concept to life!
>
> Get feedback from your partner / end-user as you build.

Questions to ask:

- What do you think this is?
- How would you use it?
- How would you improve it?
- Will this be able to meet your need?

-
-
-
-

Feedback:

PHYSICAL PROTOTYPES
- PROTOTYPE DELIVERABLE EXAMPLE

Prototype physical spaces and products using cardboards, paper and other craftable items

WIREFRAMES
– PROTOTYPE DELIVERABLE EXAMPLE
Prototype online or mobile interaction design using paper wireframes

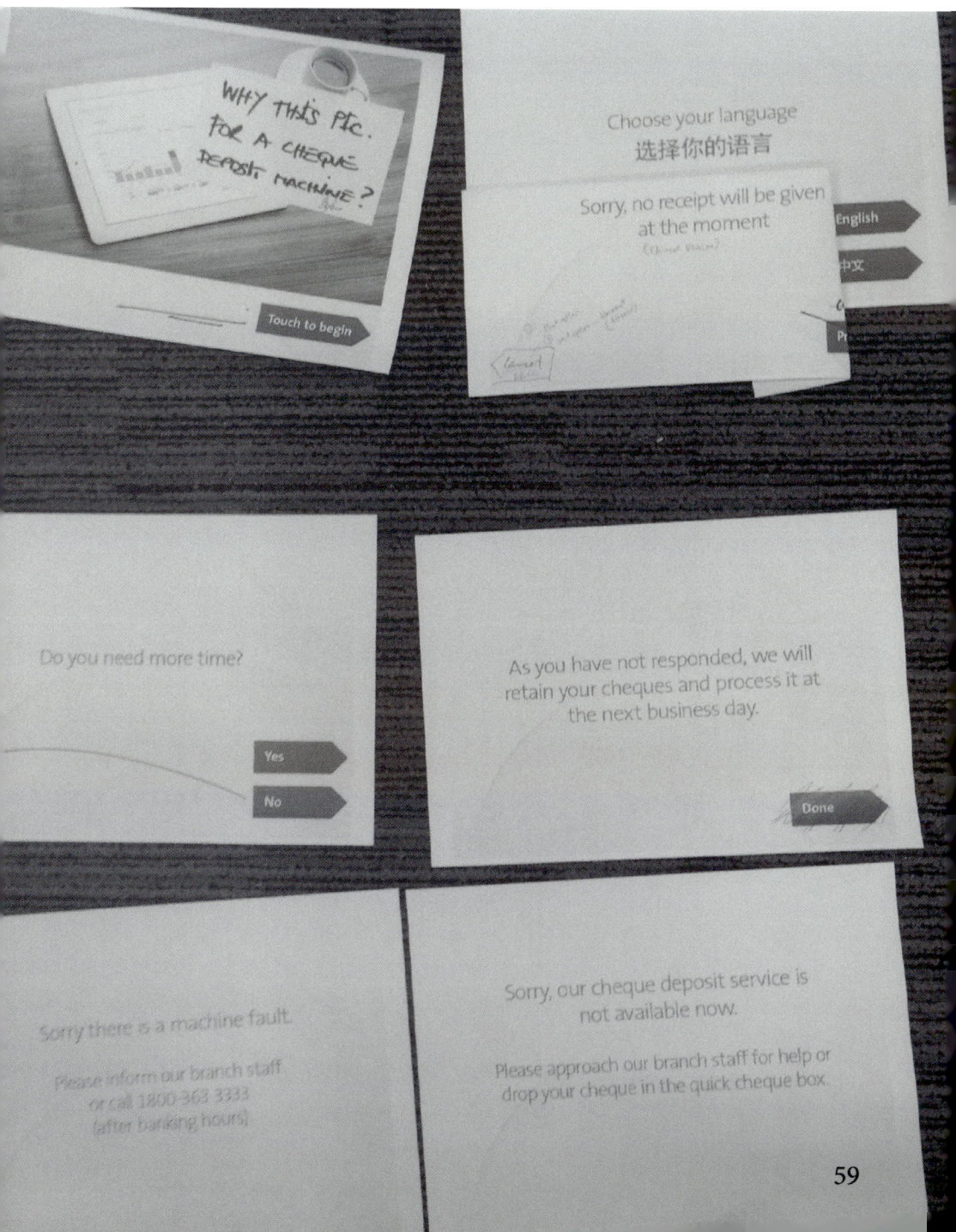

59

STORYBOARDS
- PROTOTYPE DELIVERABLE TEMPLATE
Prototype service or experience related processes using storyboarding or roleplays

	Scene 1	Dialogue	Action
	Scene 2	Dialogue	Action
		Dialogue	Action

CHAPTER 2 — DESIGN ACTION PLAN

5. TEST PHASE

Objective:

Testing is part of an iterative phase of the design thinking process that provides you with feedback, based on rigorous testing of the prototype. The purpose of testing is to learn what works, and what doesn't and then iterate. This means going back to your prototype and modifying it, based on feedback from the users. Testing ensures that you come back to the essential core of design thinking - empathy of users and designing for their needs.

Activities:

User testing
Observation
Picture-taking
Evaluation
discussion

Tools to use:

Briefing checklist
Interview checklist
Observation checklist
Prototypes to test
(from Prototype)

Deliverables:

List of user feedback
Observation
Evaluation map
Proposed refinement

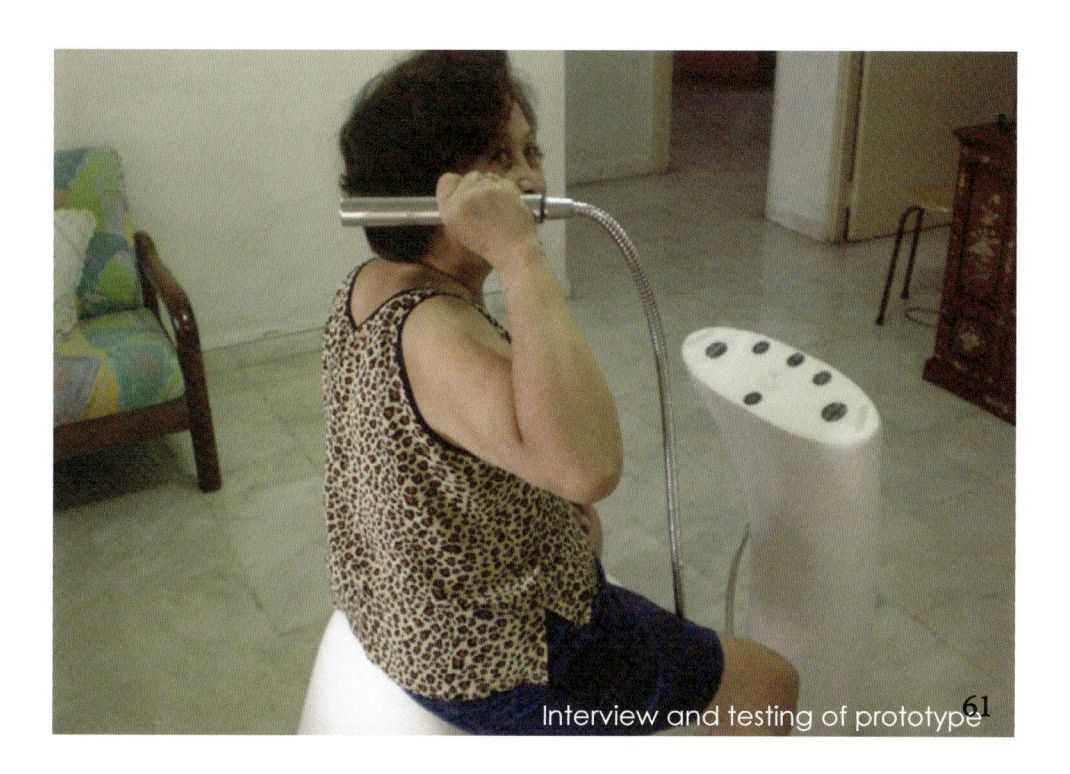

Interview and testing of prototype

QUICK TEST ACTIVITY - 14 MINS
Time to test your prototypes with users!

You would have a couple of prototypes of Wearable Technology which you can test with users.

Show your prototypes and allow your users to understand and perceive your ideas.

Think of questions to ask and get feedback from them - do not be afraid of criticism!

Feedback / refinement of selected concept:

Evaluate your prototype or ideas.

USER FEEDBACK TEMPLATE
- TEST PHASE DELIVERABLE

Test your prototype by getting feedback from users

Customer profile / background

Pros of concept / prototype

Cons of concept / prototype

Any other feedback

PROTOTYPE EVALUATION TEMPLATE
- TEST PHASE DELIVERABLE

Evaluate your prototype by comparing them using a set of evaluation criterias

Evaluation Criteria	Prototype A	Prototype B	Prototype C	Prototype D
Functionality				
Cost				
Aesthetics				
Usability				
Maintenance				
XYZ				

SUMMARY POINTS

The design thinking action plan is a framework that contains a series of action phases that execute the design thinking process.

Design thinking action plan is made of 5 phases:
1. Empathise
2. Define
3. Ideate
4. Prototype
5. Test

There are 5 distinct characteristics of the design thinking action plan.

Each action phase has specific objective, activities, tools and deliverables in order to proceed. Activities and deliverables will be discussed further in the next few chapters.

"INSANITY IS DOING THE SAME THING OVER AND OVER AGAIN AND EXPECTING DIFFERENT RESULTS."

−EINSTEIN, INVENTOR

CHAPTER 3

5 THINKING MINDSETS

CHAPTER 3
5 THINKING MINDSETS

Designers will openly share their design process but they usually do not share their mindsets. Nor do they normally share how their framework works.

Why?

This is because design thinking is so ingrained that it has become second nature. These traits and habits have been acquired and honed professionally for several years, and they assume everyone thinks the way they do.

Some of you might feel frustrated and confused when you do the design action plan, but I urge you not give up so quickly. A Stanford University psychologist, Carol Dweck, did decades of research on achievement and success, and came to the conclusion that mindset was the most important factor.

People who had a "growth mindset" believe that abilities can be acquired and honed, with hard work and dedication. Mindset was the key difference in successful people.

Here are the 5 Mindsets of design thinking:

1. Think Users First
2. Ask the Right Questions
3. Believe You can Draw
4. Commit to Explore
5. Prototype to Test

These mindsets are not to be confused with the 5 action phases, even though they are inexplicably related. You need all 5 mindsets in order for the whole the design process to run, and not using one mindset for each phase!

Without the proper mindsets, the action plan is just a theory.

SUMMARY OF THE 5 MINDSETS

Mindsets:	Need to cultivate:	Traits to follow:	Trait to avoid:
1. Think Users First	THINK- Brain to understand and put user's needs above every thing else when designing	• Step into the shoes of your customers • Have empathy on users and stakeholders	Think that you know best about your customer and putting business needs first
2. Ask The Right Questions	SAY- Mouth to ask the questions to uncover deep lying issues of the project	• Like to challenge the status quo rebelliously • Able to ask the right questions- even to your boss	Follow your management's decision and conform to red tapes
3. Believe You Can Draw	BELIEVE- Soul to believe and be confident in drawing and facilitating your ideas to your audience	• Draw and sketch instead of typing an email • Like to collaborate in multi-disciplinary meetings instead of working in silo	Afraid of people criticizing your drawing
4. Commit To Ideate	FEEL- Heart to commit in always exploring and searching for innovative ideas to solve a problem	• Look at the big picture and think holistically • Generate many new ideas and not afraid to share	Thinking that one solution is enough
5. Prototype To Test	ACT- Hands to work on creating tangible ideas to test with users by prototyping	• Find and reiterate alternatives to approach your desired goals • Willing to fail early and often	Launch a solution without prototyping and testing

ANATOMY OF A DESIGN THINKER

In Mindset: The New Psychology of Success, Stanford psychologist Carol Dweck, writes that our beliefs, both conscious and unconscious, can shape and impact nearly everything that we do.

She writes, "For twenty years, my research has shown that the view you adopt for yourself profoundly affects the way you lead your life. It can determine whether you become the person you want to be and whether you accomplish the things you value. How does this happen? How can a simple belief have the power to transform your psychology and, as a result, your life?"

Therefore, your mindsets affect how you **think, say, feel, believe and act,** and ultimately create traits, habits and a lifestyle in the way you work as a professional.

You can acquire and apply design thinking in the course of your work, even without being a professional design thinker or designer.

The 5 thinking mindsets will give you to holistic view of a design thinker, and will help you think, say, feel, believe and act like one.

How should you THINK?
Think Users First

What should you SAY?
Ask the Right Question

How should you FEEL?
Commit to Ideate

How should you ACT?
Prototype to Test

What should you BELIEVE IN?
Believe You Can Draw

MINDSET 1 - THINK USERS FIRST (HOW SHOULD YOU THINK?)

How you ever had a gadget that was reliable, intuitive, and so easy-to-use, that you didn't even have to read the instructions? Has the product met, and even exceeded your expectations?

Chances are, a great deal of design thinking went into its making. The team imagined that they themselves were the customers, and spent a great deal of time beta-testing every aspect of the product.

Requirement:

You need to cultivate your mind to keep thinking users first. A design thinker in every project will constantly make sure that the team will put the end users, or the customer, first in all design decisions.

Traits to follow:

- Constantly ask about what customers/end users will think
- Check back all design decisions with the customers/end users
- Step into the shoes of the customers
- Be constantly engaged with the end users
- Be proactive in making positive refinements for the benefit of the customers
- Focus your attention and efforts on solving customers' problems, rather than on business objectives

Traits to avoid:

- Stuck in your office cubicle and not interacting with a single customer/end user
- Ignore customer feedback
- Blindly following what the company told you to do, and not checking with the end user/ customer first
- Focus on business objectives more than solving customer's problems
- Think that the customer can be trained

1

2

> "ABOVE ALL ELSE, ALIGN WITH CUSTOMERS. WIN WHEN THEY WIN. WIN ONLY WHEN THEY WIN."
>
> – JEFF BEZOS, BUSINESS MAGNATE AND ENTREPRENEUR

MINDSET 2 - ASK THE RIGHT QUESTIONS (WHAT SHOULD YOU SAY?)

In his bestseller "Kitchen Confidential", celebrity chef and TV host Anthony Bourdain wrote about his mentor, a man he dubbed "Bigfoot".

Bigfoot spent a great deal of time trying to figure how to make his bars and restaurants operate efficiently. For example, he laid out the items in the storeroom in the same order as the checklist. He also installed hot water hoses by the sink, so that his staff could quickly dump ice in and melt it at closing time.

He did all these asking the right questions. "How can I help my staff be more productive? What can I do make things run faster, better and more efficiently?"

Requirement:

You need to cultivate your mouth to ask the right questions. In every project, a design thinker will need to ask the right questions first, to help the stakeholders and team-mates understand and define project objectives well. Asking the right questions to the end users will help to uncover underlying issues or problems to solve.

If you are not insightful enough to ask the right questions, you will slow everything down and be ineffective - and not able to create effective and meaningful progression in projects.

Traits to follow:

- Like to challenge the status quo and the "normal" way of doing things
- Able to ask the right questions - even to your boss
- Be curious and find out how things work
- Always find out the underlying motivation beneath the reason

Traits to avoid:

- Following your boss's decision blindly without asking questions
- Conform to constraints, legacy and red tape without any discussion
- Agree to everything that others say
- Not finding out why users/customers say what they say

"THE GREATEST CHALLENGE TO ANY THINKER IS STATING THE PROBLEM IN A WAY THAT WILL ALLOW A SOLUTION."

- BERTRAND RUSSELL, PHILOSOPHER

MINDSET 3 - BELIEVE YOU CAN DRAW (WHAT YOU SHOULD BELIEVE IN?)

Most people are visual creatures. We process information based on what we see. An estimated 65 percent of people are visual learners, according to the Social Science Research Network.

When we are able to visualize something, it will greatly improve our understanding of it.

Requirement:

You need to believe in the benefits of drawing. In every project, a design thinker will need to believe that he/she can draw, so that he/she can inspire others to do the same.

I have to say it once and for all – you do not have to be Picasso! You do not need to draw well to be a design thinker!

You just need to visualize correctly so that you can convey your message and story well. Drawing is the language of a design thinker.

Traits to follow:

- Draw or sketch instead of typing an email
- Able to look at the big picture and think holistically
- Visualize discussions on the board during meetings
- Facilitate and encourage others to draw

Traits to avoid:

- Not picking up a pen to draw
- Afraid that people will criticise your drawing

1

2

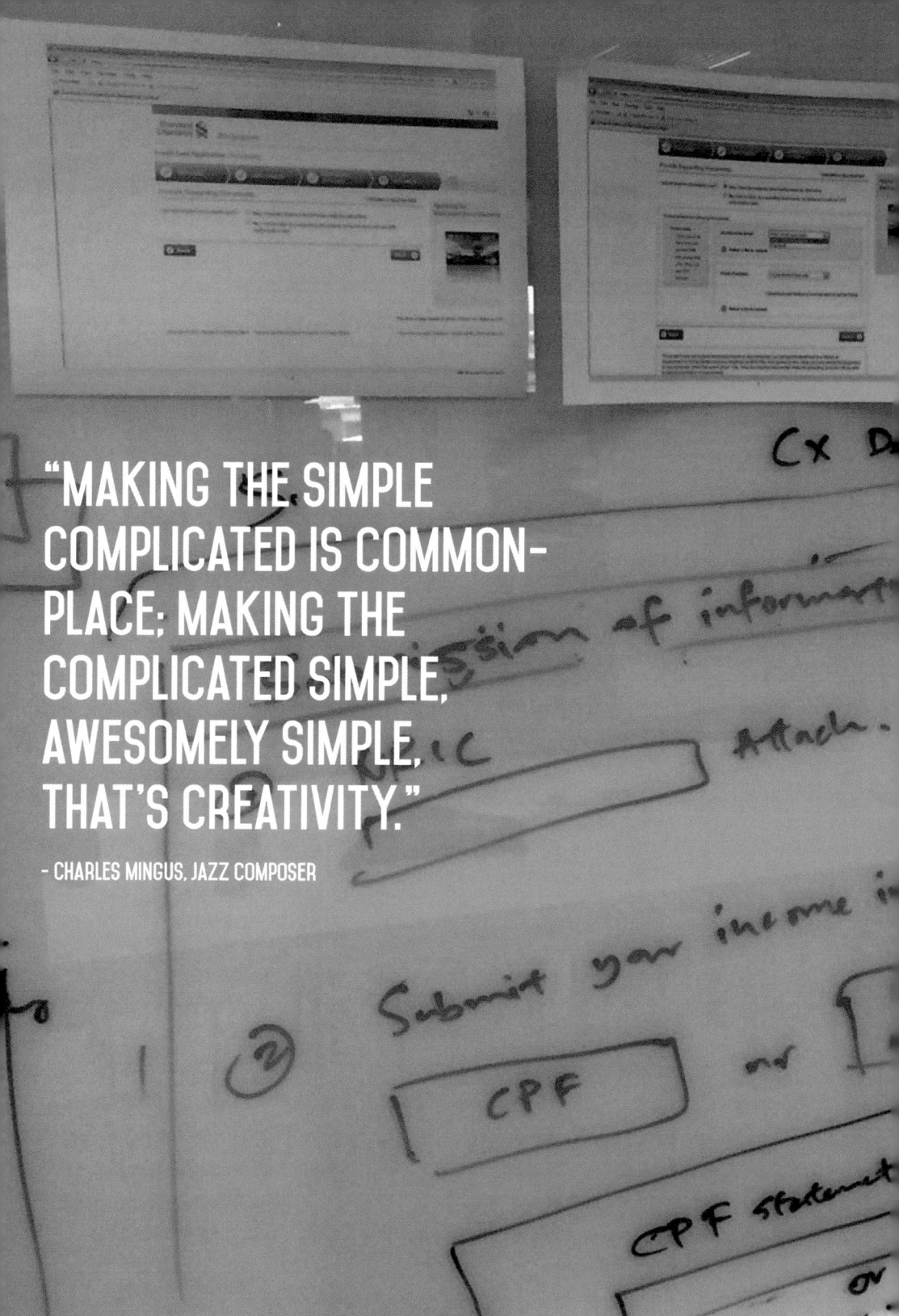

> "MAKING THE SIMPLE COMPLICATED IS COMMONPLACE; MAKING THE COMPLICATED SIMPLE, AWESOMELY SIMPLE, THAT'S CREATIVITY."
>
> – CHARLES MINGUS, JAZZ COMPOSER

MINDSET 4 - COMMIT TO EXPLORE (HOW SHOULD YOU FEEL?)

His mind (Thomas Edison) was dominated by one idea, to leave no stone unturned, to exhaust every possibility.
  - Nikola Tesla

A love of problem solving, figuring how things work – these are wonderful traits to have as a design thinker. It is not like an administrative job or accounting. You open your mind to new ideas, possibilities and let the imagination flow. A design thinker's job is never boring. In fact, it's a lot of fun.

Requirement:

You need to cultivate the heart to explore. In every project, a design thinker will need to commit to explore and think out of the box, look for solutions that are usually not thought of before. To explore all possibilities is the core foundation of a design thinker, and without it there is no divergence and no basis for innovation and creativity. It is basically solving a maths problem - where's the fun and creativity in that?

Traits to follow:

- Always realize that there is more than one solution to a problem
- Create many ideas and concepts – it doesn't matter whether they are feasible
- Constantly brainstorm ideas with teammates
- Involve in co-creation and collaborative activities
- Constantly learn from the mistakes and experiences of others
- Receive inspiration like a sponge
- Share ideas with everyone

Traits to avoid:

- Following your boss's decision blindly without asking questions
- Conform to constraints, legacy and red tape without any discussion
- Agree to everything that others say
- Ignore feedback from the users/customers

1

2

"A DESIGNER KNOWS HE HAS ACHIEVED PERFECTION NOT WHEN THERE IS NOTHING LEFT TO ADD, BUT WHEN THERE IS NOTHING LEFT TO TAKE AWAY."

- ANTOINE DE-SAINT-EXUPERY, WRITER AND POET

MINDSET 5 - PROTOTYPE TO TEST (HOW SHOULD YOU ACT?)

Prototyping is when you bring your idea to reality. It doesn't matter if it is crude. This is an initial mock-up, not the finalized product about to launch into the marketplace.

Prototyping is about experimenting and learning by doing. Prototyping is about failing quickly and cheaply - if one does not work, throw it away and try it again. The importance of this stage is to test the functionality of your design. Is there a problem? If so, what can I do to fix it?

Requirement:

You need to cultivate the hands to test out prototypes, so don't be afraid to get them dirty! A design thinker will need to build more and talk less in every project - always see the need to visualize and build to convey concepts and solutions in a quick and decisive way.

Traits to follow:

- Always have tools ready on your desk or meeting tables to build stuff
- Think of everything as an experiment
- Believe in testing solutions quickly and cheaply
- Refrain from looking into details when prototyping
- Believe in quick iteration and building from user feedback
- Be mentally prepared that not everyone will agree with your idea

Traits to avoid:

- Spending too much time on perfecting a solution
- Afraid of failing the first time
- Refuse to ask for feedback on your ideas
- Spending money to launch a solution immediately without testing
- Leaving everything to the last minute to test
- Too biased and protective of your ideas

1

2

" IT IS ABOUT DESIGNING AND PROTOTYPING AND MAKING. WHEN YOU SEPARATE THOSE, I THINK THE FINAL RESULT SUFFERS."

JONATHAN IVE, CHIEF DESIGNER OF APPLE

SUMMARY POINTS

The secret of the design thinker are actually the mindsets.

The thinking mindsets of Design Thinking is made of 5 mindsets:

1. Think Users First
2. Ask the Right Questions
3. Believe You can Draw
4. Commit to Explore
5. Prototype to Test

"DESIGN MUST REFLECT PRACTICAL AND AESTHETIC IN BUSINESS BUT ABOVE ALL... GOOD DESIGN MUST PRIMARILY SERVE PEOPLE"

–THOMAS J WATSON, INDUSTRIALIST

CHAPTER 4

THINK USERS FIRST

CHAPTER 4
THINK USERS FIRST

You need to cultivate your brain to keep thinking users first.

One of the key design projects that shaped my thinking was the design of a set of games for dementia patients. Our team went to over 12 dementia centre in Singapore, did research and talked to staff, caregivers and patients on what activities that is helpful to them.

Dementia patients have a particular set of needs that is different from people that are well and able. Naturally the games they play will be different. Designing card games for dementia requires a lot of empathy and understanding- by stepping into their shoes and thinking about how they feel. It is very challenging but it allows me to understand one thing- think users first.

Without thinking users first, you will not be able to design an effective product/ service, neither will the product you design be relevant or useful to the end user. It will not work despite any effort. I strongly recommend you to go slow to go fast- spend time understanding your users first so that you can make fast decisions later.

Understanding and empathizing customer needs should be at the centre of every successful business. However good your product or service is, no-one will purchase if it does not meet their needs or they don't believe in it. Hence, by understanding customer and user needs, you don't have to persuade too hard to deliver success.

In this chapter, you will learn:
What are your user's inherent needs?
How do you empathise your user?
What do you need to know from your user/customer?
How to interview your users effectively?
What is a persona and how to use it?
What is the empathy map and how to use it?

WHAT ARE YOUR USER'S INHERENT NEEDS?

Whenever we design something, we must first identify how is your product/service be able to meet the needs of your user. Research have found and created a list of basic user needs that serve as a motivation for him or her to take buying action.

10 key areas that users pursue improvement/growth in:

Wealth

Security

Being Liked

Status and Prestige

Health and Fitness

Praise and Recognition

Power and Popularity

Knowledge

Love and Companionship

Self-Actualization

If at least one of these inherent user needs are met, the product/ service that you are designing is deemed to be of value. Hence, it is more likely that the user will purchase your product/ service.

HOW DO YOU EMPATHIZE YOUR USER?

Observe
Watch your user in action and take note of non-verbal cues and body language.

Meet
Visit your user or arrange a meet-up with him to find out more about his life, workplace or even his home. You will develop empathy into the context or situation he is in.

Ask questions
Ask non-leading and open-ended questions that find out more.

Listen
Allow your user to tell his story.

ASK QUESTIONS- WHAT DO YOU NEED TO KNOW FROM YOUR USER/CUSTOMER?

It is important to know how to ask the right questions, below are some guidelines that you may your questions along:

Who they are
Individuals- What is your age? What is your marital status and occupation? What are your interests?
Companies- What kind of business and what size?

What they do
Individuals- What do you do at work? What did you study? What do you do during your free time?
Companies- What is the usual routine and operations? Who do you target?

Why they buy
Find out why customers buy a product/service, write down their needs to the benefits your business can offer.

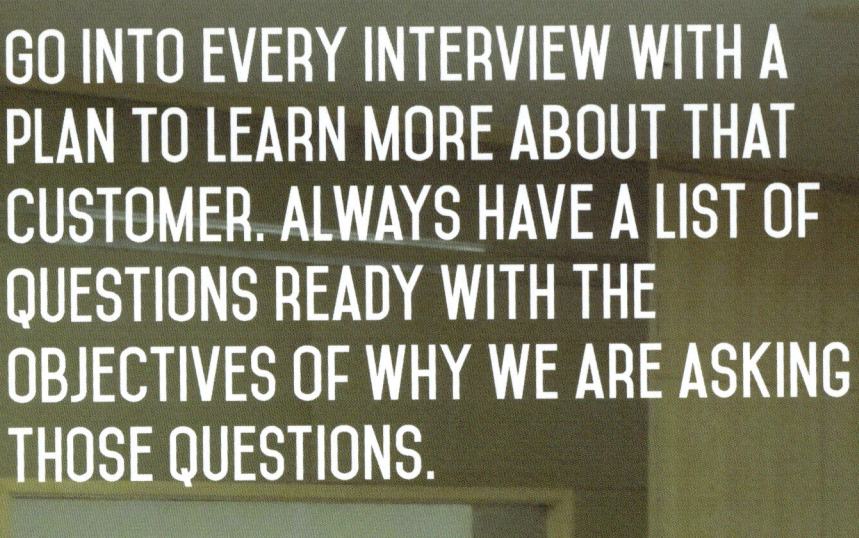

GO INTO EVERY INTERVIEW WITH A PLAN TO LEARN MORE ABOUT THAT CUSTOMER. ALWAYS HAVE A LIST OF QUESTIONS READY WITH THE OBJECTIVES OF WHY WE ARE ASKING THOSE QUESTIONS.

PREPARE FOR THE INTERVIEW

How they buy
Find out how customers go through the channels to purchase something. For example, some people prefer to buy from a website, while others prefer a face-to-face meeting.

What makes them feel good about buying
Find out what makes customers tick so that you understand your value proposition.

What they expect of you
Find out what are delighters or pain points of your product/service. For example, if your customers expect reliable delivery and you don't disappoint them, you stand to gain repeat business.

What they think about you
Find out what are the impressions/service that your customer have towards your product/service. If your customers enjoy dealing with you, they're likely to buy more

STEPS TO TAKE FOR PREPARING AN INTERVIEW

Prepare for the interview
Go into every interview with a plan to learn more about that customer- and with this you need to be prepared. Always have a list of questions ready with the objectives of why we are asking those questions.

Use the USER FEEDBACK example in the next page if you need guidance.

Start a conversation not an inquisition.
While you know what you're trying to find out and you know the type of questions you're going to ask, interrogating a customer with an endless stream of questions is not recommended.

Let it be a conversation, allow the customer to be at ease and his story to take centre stage. Let your question emerge out from the conversation- when the customer talking on a relevant topic, you need to be quick to interject with your question. Listen intently to your customer and pause to think about what he said, and then decide where you want to conversation to go.

Introduce non-leading, open-ended questions.

Ideally, your questions should be open-ended, meaning that they can't be answered with a single word. The best way to ensure you're asking open-ended questions is to start the questions with "How", What" or "Why"

Don't worry about asking a question that is "too open-ended." If your question isn't specific enough, the customer will ask you to clarify. And then you're already in a conversation, which is half the battle. That is why you need to equip with question objectives, which will help assure your customer on the reason why you ask the question.

1

2

3

EXAMPLE OF USER FEEDBACK

Customer profile:

Lim Mei Ling, 53
Housewife
Existing customer of ABC Bank
Other banking relationship with XYZ Bank
Has 2 children
Likes to trade during free time
Dislike internet banking

Questions to ask:

List of questions	Why do we ask these questions?
• Have you seen / aware of this credit card?	• Understand awareness level
• What do you think of its benefits?	• Understand if the benefits are relevant to customer
• How is it compared to other credit cards?	• Understand how it is compared among other competitors

User feedback:

Observations and feedback	Insights / Actions
• Generally unable to recall where she has seen the card	• Advertising visibility / stickiness could be improved
• Frowned and talked about the painful application process of the card	• Application process may be painful for customer
• Emphasizes the benefit of groceries rebate	• Could strengthen and shout groceries rebates in marketing

WHAT IS A PERSONA ?

A persona is a description of a fictional person that represents one target segment that you are developing a product/service for. You may create more than one personas for your consideration of different target segments.

For example, if you are creating a new lunchbox for kids- you may need one persona of a kid who needs to use this lunchbox and another persona of a busy parent who needs to pack his lunch with the lunchbox.

HOW TO CREATE A PERSONA?

Like every design project, creating a persona should be collaboratively. Involving the stakeholders and other team members increases the accuracy of the persona and creates a level of awareness about the users that helps the team align around them.

An even better practice is to interview users, use the data collected to validate and refine the personas.

Use the PERSONA example if you need guidance.

You can build your persona according to:
Profile
Character
Behavior
Expectations
Motivations
Needs and Goals
Challenges / Opinions to your topic

BENEFITS OF PERSONA

Identify opportunities and product gaps to drive strategy

Provide a quick and cheap way to test, validate and prioritize ideas throughout development

Give focus to projects by building a common understanding of customers across teams

Help development teams empathize with users, including their behaviors, goals, and expectations

Serve as a reference tool that can be used from strategy through to implementation

EXAMPLE OF **PERSONA**

Name:
Johnathan Lim, 38

Profile / Lifestyle:
Lawyer, single
Likes to play golf once a week
Own an apartment in Serangoon

Characteristics
Ambitious
Knowledgeable
Financially savvy

Goals / Ambitions
Wants to invest money for his retirement
Gunning for promotion to Senior Counsel this year

Behaviors / Habits
Impatient
Prim and proper
Don't take no for an answer

Fears / Challenges
Not working well with colleagues
Unable to find time with family

Influencers and Activities
Uncle, who is also a lawyer
Golf

WHAT IS AN EMPATHY MAP?

Empathy map is another method of documenting your customers. While personas is revealing more about the person, empathy map is revealing more about how the person feel about a particular topic.
You may create the empathy map based on co-creation with stakeholders or from interview with customers.

Use the EMPATHY MAP example if you need guidance.

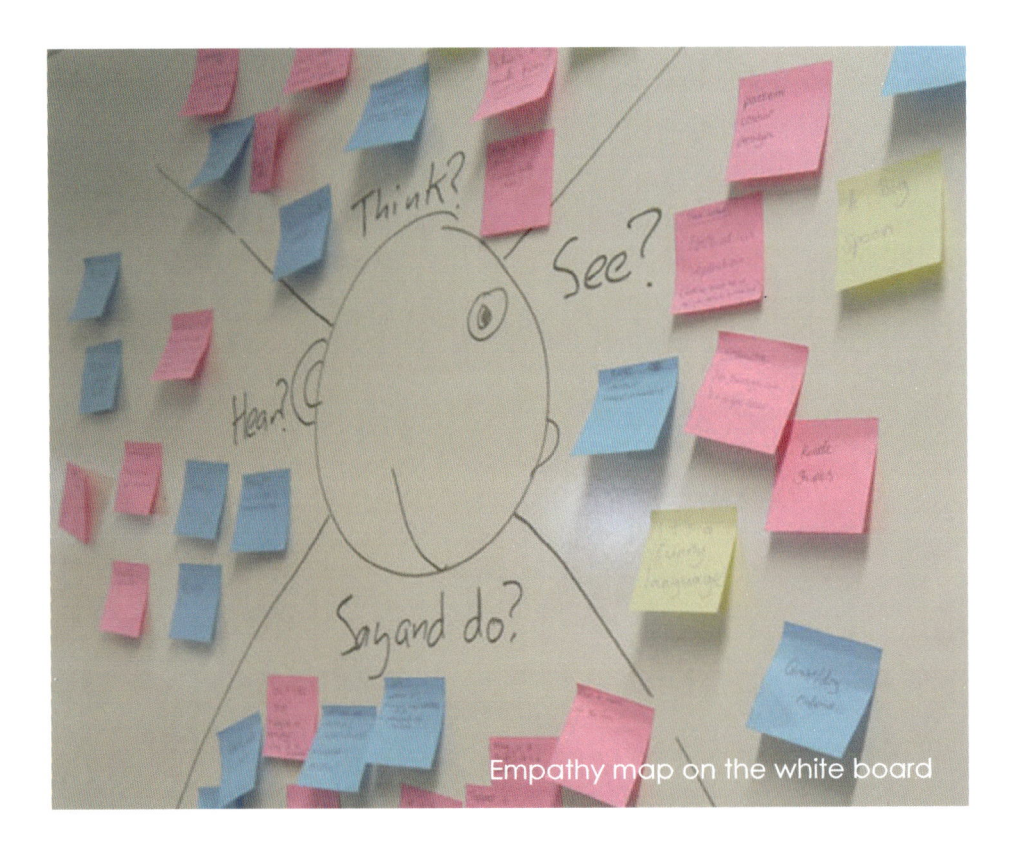

Empathy map on the white board

EXAMPLE OF **EMPATHY MAP**

Think and Feel

Thinks fast food outlet near the school is unhealthy

Hear

Understand that fast food is the leading cause of obesity

Customer

Concerned Parent

See

Many children goes to the outlet to buy fast food

Say and Do

Complains to the school management

Pain

Concern that her child will be influenced

Gain

Nothing to gain

SUMMARY POINTS

You need to cultivate your brain to keep thinking users first.

You need to understand the 10 inherent needs of the users before designing any product/ service.

There are 4 steps you need to take to empathise your user.

It is important to take step to prepare and ask the right questions when interviewing a user.

You can create a persona or an empathy map to understand the user- to find out their profile or their feedback on the topic respectively.

"I PREFER DESIGN BY EXPERTS - BY PEOPLE WHO KNOW WHAT THEY ARE DOING"

-DON NORMAN, DESIGN THINKER

CHAPTER 5

ASK THE RIGHT QUESTIONS

CHAPTER 5
ASK THE RIGHT QUESTIONS

You need to cultivate your mouth to ask the right questions.

Perhaps nothing is more important in the design thinking process than the art of asking the right questions. Questions are lightsticks- they illuminate things that were previously vague, untrue or undiscovered. You will realise by asking the right questions- you will empathize your end-users better, define clear project objectives with stakeholders and create better solutions.

The Head of Innovation of P&G once told me that in order to ensure that their innovation successful, they need to solve the correct problem correctly. If they are able to solve their customer's problem or meet his needs, chances are that their innovation will be a success.

So how to "solve the correct problem correctly"? The key to find the correct problem is to ask the right questions. We need to ask the right questions to find out more from our customers, stakeholders and management for details that will be useful to define the problem. The key is to be inquisitive and challenging the status quo by asking questions.

One of the key mindset of a design thinker is to know the different type of questions and how to use them at different situations across the design thinking process.

In this chapter, you will learn:
Why do you need to ask the right questions?
What are the different type of questions?
Who will you ask?
What should you do when a project comes to you?
How to align stakeholders in meetings?

WHY DO YOU NEED TO ASK THE RIGHT QUESTIONS?

Effective questions help you:

- Empathise your end-users and stakeholders
- Connect and collaborate with more aligned objectives
- Gather better information
- Examine and define the problem more effectively
- Increase your persuasion and influence
- Improve your negotiation skills
- Reduce potential for mistakes or miscommunication
- Discover potential issues and opportunities

WHAT ARE THE DIFFERENT TYPE OF QUESTIONS?

There are 5 different type of questions that you can apply. These questions are most commonly applied during the DEFINE PHASE of the design thinking process- where you and your stakeholders, including the bosses score it out on what the project is about.

Note that these questions positioned differently from questions to ask of your end-user/ customers (see Think Users First)

Opening questions

The idea behind an opening question is to understand the context and options, assess the situation, provoke thought and possibilities and jumpstart the brain.

What is the problem we are trying to solve?
What are we looking at?
What kind of things do we want to explore?
What are the problem areas in this?

Navigating questions

Navigating questions helps you to assess or adjust the course of the meeting while the discussion is ongoing. It helps to assure and bring the stakeholders together.

Are we on the right track?
Is this useful?
Did I understand this correctly?
Are we aligned on all this?
Does anyone have any questions?

Examining questions

Examining questions challenges and focus into details of the project. It helps to facilitate and define the project deeper by quantifying and qualifying it.

What is it made of?
How does it work?
How much of it are we selling at the moment?
What percentage increase in sales are we trying to achieve in 2 years?
Can you give me an example of this situation?
What happens after that?

Experimenting questions

Experimenting questions, unlike examining questions, are more divergent in nature. It invokes the imagination and possibilities. These questioning are especially useful during ideation sessions.

What if we did this using plan B?
What else could we use this?
What is missing over here?
What if we are wrong?
How would we handle if we are operating like a school?

Closing questions

Closing questions puts the tyre on the road and brings the project into a pragmatic and realistic state. These are crucial set of questions as it defines the action plan and steps to take.

How can we prioritize these ideas?
What are the action steps?
Who is going to do what?
What should we see in the next 2 weeks?
Which one will bring us forward?

WHO SHOULD YOU ASK QUESTIONS?

Customers / End-users

With customers and end-users, you approach them with a learning attitude and never think that you know best about the topic. Before meeting with them, you should prepare a set of empathy questions (Pg XX) with the objectives of why you are asking those questions.

Questions could be like:
How would you do this?
Tell me more about this?
What is your feeling about this?

Stakeholders

Stakeholders are your allies and partners in a project and you do want to align by asking critical questions to like:
What is in it for you?
What's your objective?
What's your role in this?

Management

Usually conversations between the management and working group are lacking because people do not dare to ask the right questions. This will not be productive as projects will run based on assumptions on what the management wants and not what they require.

For management, you may want to ask high-level questions like:
- Where do you see this going?
- What are the problems?
- What is considered a success?
- Any time/budget constraints?

Vendors

Relationship with vendors are equally important as the stakeholders, because ultimately they will be the ones delivering the product/ service.

For vendors, we have to ask work-related questions upfront:
- Are you able to do it?
- Can it be done?
- How could we work together?

WHAT SHOULD YOU DO WHEN A PROJECT COMES TO YOU?

You have to be very sharp and skilful whenever a new project comes to you- it does not mean every project that comes to you is worth a shot. Sometimes, the multi-million dollar answer could be: "Nope, I don't think we should pursue this." And explain the rationale.

Obviously, we have to be tactical about this because the person that comes to you might be your boss, an important stakeholder or a lucrative client. In order to deal with this, you have to understand that every project initiation comes already with something- mainly an idea, a solution or a problem.

When an idea comes from him:
- Always ask how does this idea come about
- Elaborate that even though you thank him for the idea, we need to identify what is the problem we are solving
- Let him focus more on the problem rather than be in love with his idea
- Let him see the need to empathize his end-users

When an solution comes from him:
- Always ask how does this solution come about
- Identify what is the problem we are solving
- Assure him that we should not get fixated on a solution, as there could be other solutions to discover
- Position yourselves as an opportunity to validate the solution- by empathizing the users

When a problem comes from him:
- Always ask how does this problem come about
- Align all stakeholders of the problem
- Build the context
- Understand the users

When a desire comes from him:
- Always understand why we need to act on this desire
- Are there any factors / pressure / external factors that motivates this action?
- Assess whether this desire is valid and always think users first

HOW TO ALIGN STAKEHOLDERS IN MEETINGS?

Usually you will be in a situation where all the stakeholders will be in a meeting, all with different agendas. Bring the problem on the table and align the stakeholders to solve the common problem. Create objectives using the DESIGN BRIEF and also find out what are the different sub-objectives do the other stakeholders want to achieve.

Build the DESIGN BRIEF early as everyone will understand the problem and the key objectives of design intent.

Define the roles of each stakeholder in a STAKEHOLDER MAP- some will be directly involved in execution, some will be in the steering committee and some will serve as a knowledge panel.

Get the stakeholders to listen to your users. Conduct CUSTOMER JOURNEY MAP in order to identify pain points, thoughts and emotions of the customer. Conduct customer labs in the presence of your stakeholders will create magic as everyone starts to step into the shoes of the customers and think along the same way.

Build CONTEXT MAP and OPPORTUNITY MAP in order to understand the situation surrounding the product or service which they are persuing.

Key is to make sure that you understand the needs of each stakeholder and their involvement.

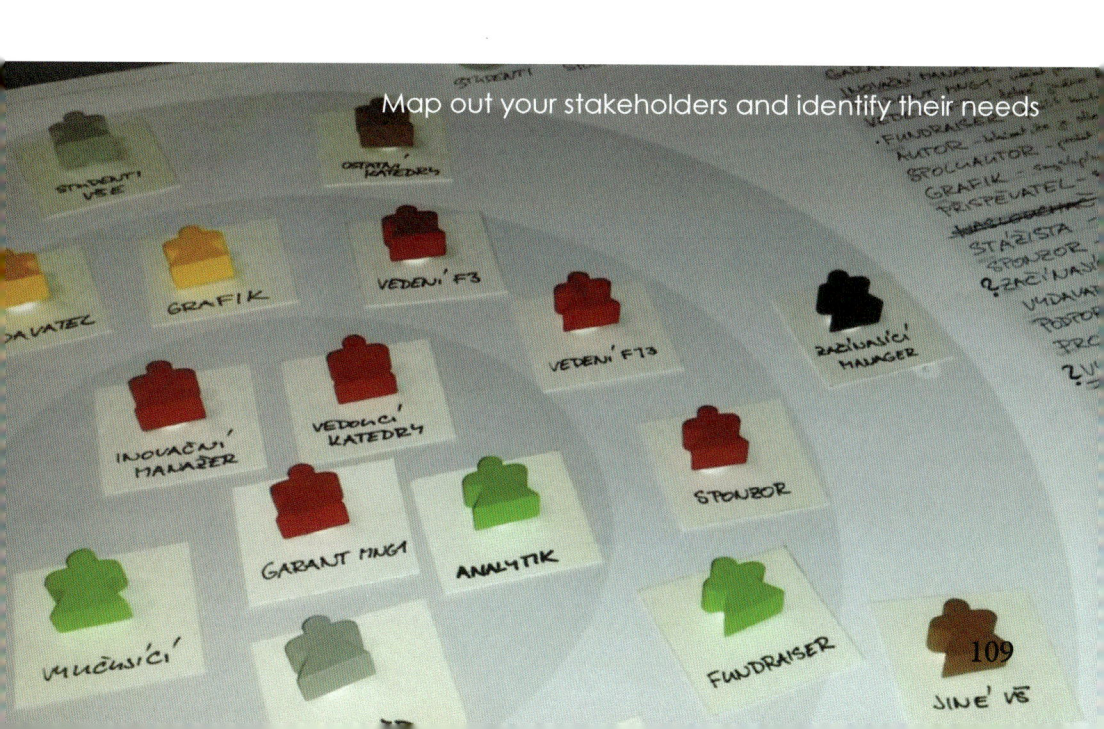

Map out your stakeholders and identify their needs

1. ALIGN STAKEHOLDERS - DESIGN BRIEF

What is it?

Design brief is a very important document and deliverable of the define phase in order to create a statement of intent on behalf of the project team. The design brief defines the problem clearly with a problem statement, based on the insights gained from user interviews and feedback.

Based on the design problem, the design brief will also define the key objective and scope of requirements of their design intent, which provides the project team with a target and reference for their efforts.

The key is to make sure that the defined problem and intent is clear and unambiguous to all the team and other stakeholders.

Key benefits

Clarify problem to be solved and design intent

Allow team to be focused and aligned

Achieve better result by comparing the design outcome with the original brief

EXAMPLE OF **DESIGN BRIEF**

User perception / feedback

- Darryl needs a fast and efficient way to track his health and fitness
- He runs/swims often and does not like to carry a phone while running/swimming

Problem statement

User could not track his fitness and health while running/swimming

Design goal / objective

How may we design a convenient and hands-free fitness and health tracking device for running/swimming?

Design requirements

- Our product / service should ....

- Track fitness and health while doing activity
- Lightweight
- Waterproof / Sweatproof
- Impact proof
- Convenient to use / Handsfree

2. ALIGN STAKHOLDERS - STAKEHOLDER MAP

What is it?

Stakeholder maps are used to document the key stakeholders and their relationship. They can include the end users, those who will benefit from the project, those who may be adversely affected, those who may hold power and those who will influence the design outcomes.

At the beginning of the Define Phase, we need to ask the right questions early to detect the stakeholders and their relationship such that it may serve as reference for the design team for design communication.

Key benefits

Clarify stakeholders and their relationship

Understand the decision-makers, influencers, executers and even the end-users.

Allow design team to discover risks from negative stakeholders and support from positive ones.

EXAMPLE OF **STAKEHOLDER MAP**

Stakeholder Map of an IT project

Vendors / Influencers

HCL
(IT Implementor)

Derrick
(Design Agency)

External stakeholders

TBD
(Steering Comm Members)

CJ
(Knowledge Panel)

Project team

Daniel (Designer)
Joyce (User PM)
David (IT PM)

Alvin
(Sales Team Lead)

Ashish
(E-business)

Faith
(Legal / Compliance)

Angela
(Marketing)

3. ALIGN STAKHOLDERS - CUSTOMER JOURNEY

What is it?

Customer journey mapping is a method of documenting and visualising the experiences the customers have with a particular product or service that your team is about to refine or improve. This includes customers thoughts and feelings at each moment of their experience as well as the touchpoint that they are interfacing with. It also includes what happens on the backend operations that is needed to make an experience happen.

This allows your team to access and analyze the interacting factors that form a customer experience.

Key benefits

Align stakeholders an overview of your customer's experience from their point of view

Identify pain points at specific moment of an experience and improve on those

Help the team to focus on specific areas rather than revamping the whole service or product experience

EXAMPLE OF CUSTOMER JOURNEY

Activity Phase	Enter Starbucks	Find Seat	Buy Coffee	Wait for Coffee	Drink Coffee
Customer Actions	Look at cafe surroundings	Walk around the cafe	Queue at the counter to be served	Wait at the counter	Seated at the table
Touchpoints	Entrance / Posters	Cafe Space	Counter / Price Display	Counter	Seat
Thoughts	Am I entering the right place?	Can I find seats?	How much is it?	How long do I have to wait?	Ah....
Emotions	+	■			
Backend Processes			Payment process	Brew the coffee	Clearing of tables

4. ALIGN STAKHOLDERS - CONTEXT MAP

What is it?

Context map is a tool and document to represent complex factors affecting the organisation or the design of the product or service. Context maps are used by designers and project managers to enable discussions on change relating to business / technological or even environmental factors. It also discusses potential target audience, trends that may arise or uncertainties and risk involved in this project.

Key benefits

Create a shared strategic vision with the team

Document knowledge existing informally within the organisation

Understand the external factors which plays in deciding and planning of the design of the product / service.

EXAMPLE OF **CONTEXT MAP**

Context Map of Motion Sensor that detects when an elderly fall.

Target users / User needs

Elderly, aged 65 and above
Living alone at home
Needs immediate attention or help if a fall happens
Children of elderly wants to be notified immediately

Technology factors

- Existing technology of motion related sensors
- To connect remotely via app related devices

Business factors

No current competitors

Trends

- Aging society
- Rise in affluent silver generation
- Increase in one person living household

Uncertainties

- Adoption rate of the elderly
- Modification of house required?
- Execution of the service

Other questions?

Any support from government community?

Other questions?

Other questions?

117

5. ALIGN STAKHOLDERS - OPPORTUNITY MAP

What is it?

Opportunity map allows comparison of any product / service that is in the market which helps to identify saturation of competitors or areas of opportunities where the designers could potentially position the product / service.

This allows all the stakeholders to identify the direction of the product or service to meet the opportunity in the market.

Key benefits

Identify area of opportunities

Identify areas of saturation and competition where the positioning of the new product / idea should be avoided

Align stakeholders with shared direction and meaning

EXAMPLE OF OPPORTUNITY MAP

Opportunity Map of Nail Salons in Singapore

Retail

Salon I

Salon J

Salon E

Salon H

Salon G

Salon B

Salon D

Mass   Exclusive

Area of opportunity

Salon A

Salon C

Salon F

Home-based

SUMMARY POINTS

You need to cultivate your mouth to keep asking the right questions.

There are 8 reasons why asking the right questions assist you in design thinking.

You can use 5 different type of questions throughout your discussion in order to ask questions effectively.

You need to understand the difference between an idea, a solution and a problem when a project comes to you.

Use various templates to align stakeholders to the same objectives.

> "THIS IS WHAT I LIKE ABOUT BEING A DESIGNER: YOU CAN'T REALLY GET IT UNTIL YOU SEE IT."
>
> —ISAAC MIZRAHI, FASHION DESIGNER

CHAPTER 6
BELIEVE YOU CAN DRAW

CHAPTER 6
BELIEVE YOU CAN DRAW

Drawing is an instinct that we all possess. We have to be taught to read and write, but we are born with the ability to learn to draw. However, this innate ability to express or communicate by drawing is underutilized, as we become more comfortable with typing emails or phone calls in design project discussions. Design projects become unproductive and incoherent, if we fail to communicate and agree by means of drawing.

When I was a young designer, I thought that I needed to sketch like a Picasso in order to impress and excel. However, compared to others in school, my drawing skills were mediocre. I was very disheartened and demotivated.

I held on to this notion until I met my boss when I was in OCBC Bank- he was one of the best design thinkers that I have ever met. While his drawings seemed amateurish, he shared this valuable insight with me, "Daniel, you draw like a Picasso, while I draw stick-men and arrows, but in the end we just do one thing - to visualize and communicate through our drawings. It doesn't matter how well you draw, it matters how well you think."

I had the technical skills to draw, but he had the self-belief that he could draw! You need to cultivate the belief that you can draw!

"I prefer drawing to talking. Drawing is faster and leaves less room for lies"
- Le Corbusier

In this chapter, you will learn:
Why should we communicate by drawing?
What is value of drawing?
What's the problem with the current mode of communication?
How to start drawing?
How to start facilitation by drawing?

WHY SHOULD WE COMMUNICATE BY DRAWING?

Drawings and pictures allow people to agree on what they see, and not what they imagine.

Words, on the other hand, leave things open for each person's interpretation and understanding. Consider this - which of these allow your stakeholders to 'see' the situation? Which one is more convincing?

Text   vs   **Picture**

Our train station
experience overcrowding
this morning.
It is very bad.

WHY SHOULD WE COMMUNICATE BY DRAWING?

Drawing saves time by replacing words to explain a particular situation.

People are able to see, understand and agree on a drawing faster than trying to interpret a paragraph of text. Consider the following:

Text
- We have four people on a red boat with a black roof and a flag drifting along the sea.
- The sea has green, orange, red and purple flying fishes.
- There is one particular flying fish that is bigger than the rest.
- There is a white seagull flying towards the big flying fish.
- 3 more birds fly across the sky.
- They are attacking the flying red ship with blue smoke.
- The sun is smiling.
- For some reasons, the sky is yellow.
- I am Alex.

vs

Drawing

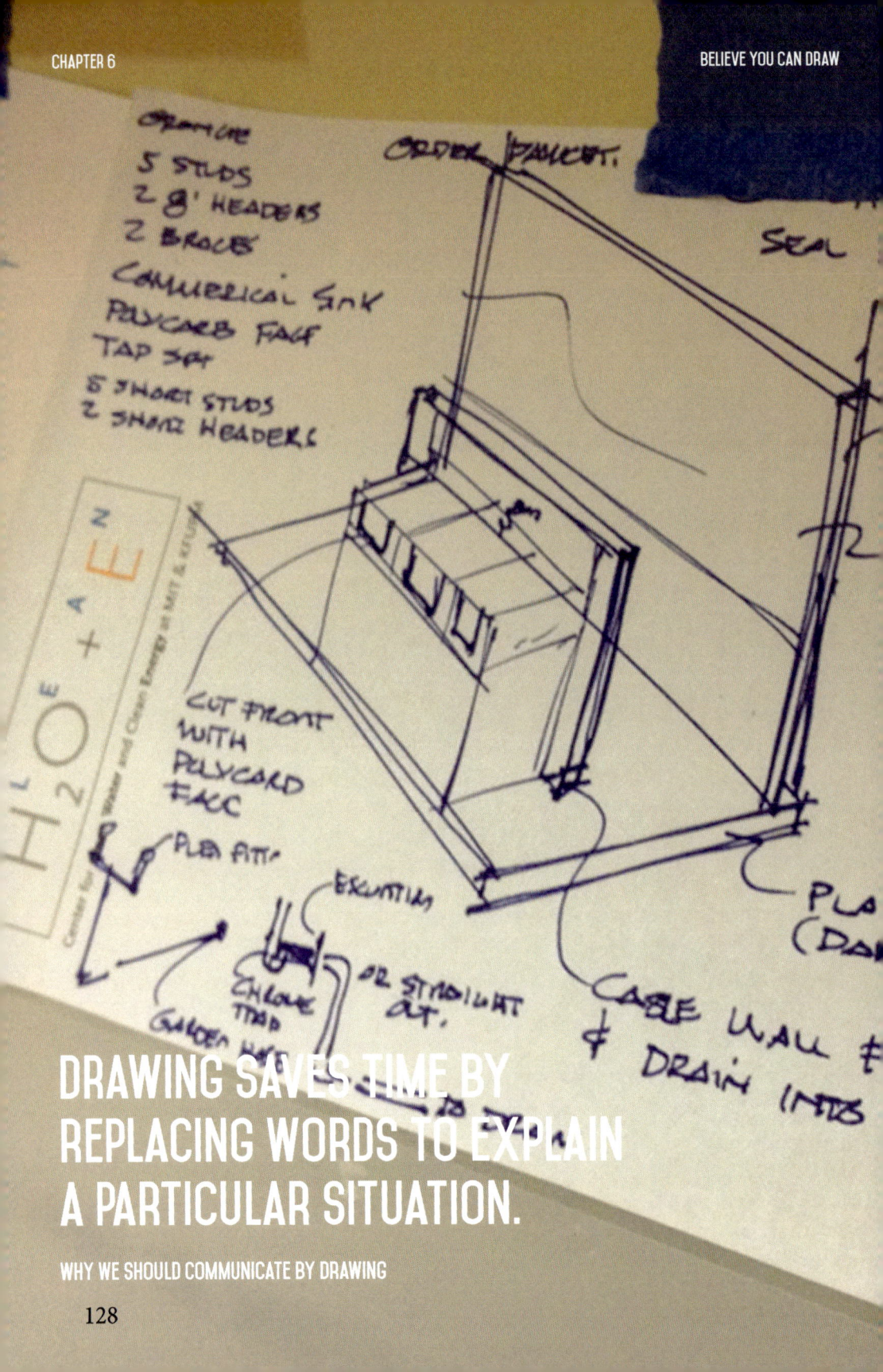

CHAPTER 6 BELIEVE YOU CAN DRAW

DRAWING SAVES TIME BY REPLACING WORDS TO EXPLAIN A PARTICULAR SITUATION.

WHY WE SHOULD COMMUNICATE BY DRAWING

WHAT IS VALUE OF DRAWING?

Drawing is a unique creative space that enables you visualize something and put it on paper. You can run through the ideas in your head, explore alternatives with less risk, and facilitate meaningful discussions and constructive criticisms:

Imagine better ideas
We do lots of drawing to help us imagine better ideas. Drawing helps us become more creative and successful.

Figure out things
We draw to figure out things that are in our heads. Drawing makes us smarter. When I make something, I often do several drawings to see how it should look or it figure out if it will even work.

Explain and give instructions
Drawing helps us explain things and give instructions. It is often much easier to understand something from a drawing than from words. Drawing a chart or a graph helps us make comparisons and choices.

Helps to remember
Drawing helps us notice and see more. As you draw something, you mentally break things down into components. If you make a very careful drawing of a real fish, you will notice all the parts of the fish – eyes, gills, fins etc. If you want to learn all the parts of anything, there is no better way.

WHAT'S THE PROBLEM WITH THE CURRENT MODE OF COMMUNICATION?

Too many people are cooped in front of their computers - typing and sending emails.

Such modes of communication are detrimental to projects as it is always a linear communication - with no discussion or co-creation. Disagreements usually take a long time to be resolved. There is misunderstanding as perception of words differs.

With design thinking, it is different. You are a team working to resolve an issue, a problem, or you are trying to create something. As peers, you need to have that free flow and exchange of ideas, feedback and criticism.

Drawing spontaneously will cultivate agreement and create common understanding, and save a lot of time in the process.

CHAPTER 6　　　　　　　　　　　　　　　　　　　　　　　　　BELIEVE YOU CAN DRAW

HOW TO START DRAWING?

A lot of people are afraid to draw, because they will be criticized that their sketches are ugly etc. There is only one solution - practice!

Go to the stationery shop and buy a few sketch books, highlighters, different colour pens, and pencils. Clip out pictures and visuals from magazines. Doodle in your free time. Get comfortable with expressing your ideas visually. Don't worry about making it look pretty, just draw!

Create your own library of visual elements.

You need to create your own set of visual library (drawings and visuals that you are comfortable with) so that in the future you are able to facilitate meetings effectively with drawings. Below are a set of drawings for your reference, and of course it is not exhaustive. Feel free to draw more pictures for yourself!

PEOPLE

Customer　Boss / Staff　Female　Male　Crowd / Group　Walking Man

People Celebrating　Staff in a Meeting　People Agreeing

EMOTIONS

Angry　Confused　Frustrated　Happy　Sick

TIME

1 PM　Future　Morning　Night　Now!

CHAPTER 6   BELIEVE YOU CAN DRAW

PLACES

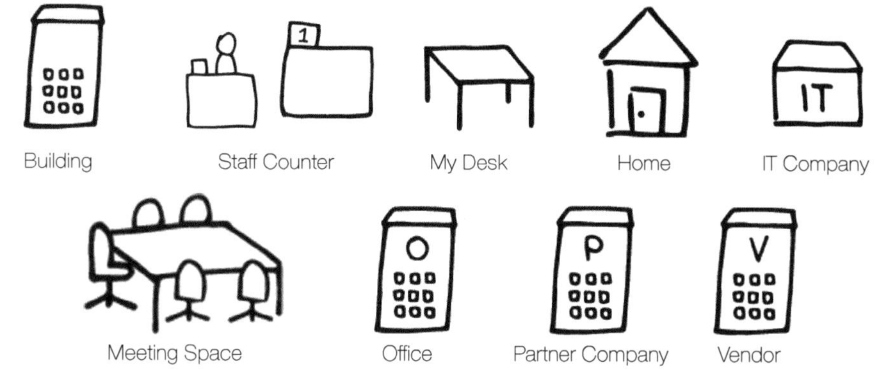

Building	Staff Counter	My Desk	Home	IT Company
Meeting Space	Office	Partner Company	Vendor	

CHANNELS

Attachment	Document	Email	Forms	Laptop / Internet	Mail
Mobile	Self-Service Kiosk	Car	Delivery		

IDENTIFIERS

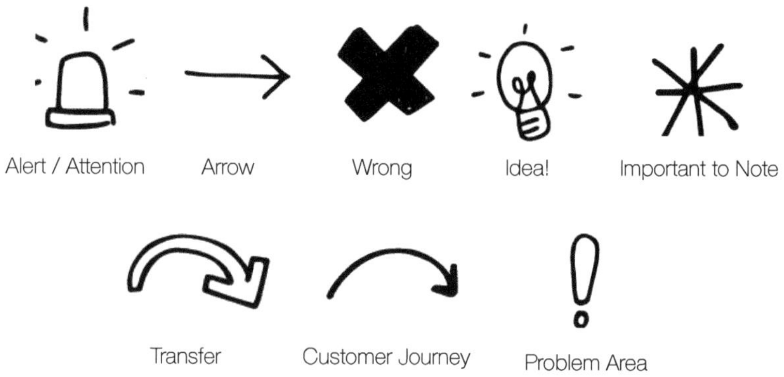

Alert / Attention	Arrow	Wrong	Idea!	Important to Note
Transfer	Customer Journey	Problem Area		

131

CHAPTER 6 BELIEVE YOU CAN DRAW

Learn how to draw a journey or a process.

It is very important to learn how to draw a journey or a process as your drawings have to represent a story or a sequence of events. This will be helpful to your audience in understanding what you are trying to explain and identify potential issues or problems through the process.

Below is the example of a customer journey in Starbucks:

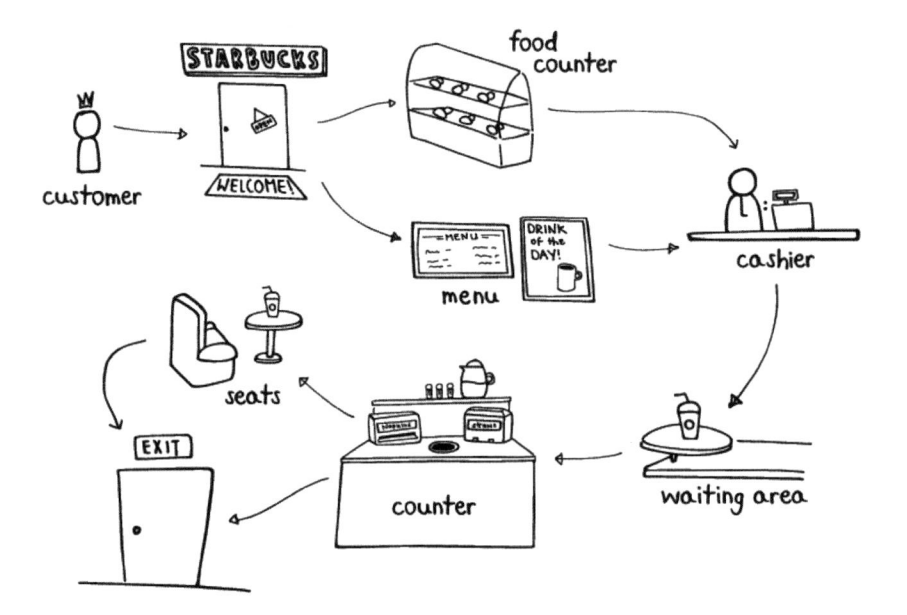

1

2

132

Learn how to draw your problem.

Drawing also allows you to articulate your problem better. This is especially useful for facilitators or design consultants to identify the problem at hand and get the rest of the stakeholders to recognize the problem. This is more impactful if the problem is created visually, so that you can discuss things more openly, and leave less room for ambiguity.

Below is the example of a typical boardroom problem in a bank:

We can visualize the problem by drawing it out:

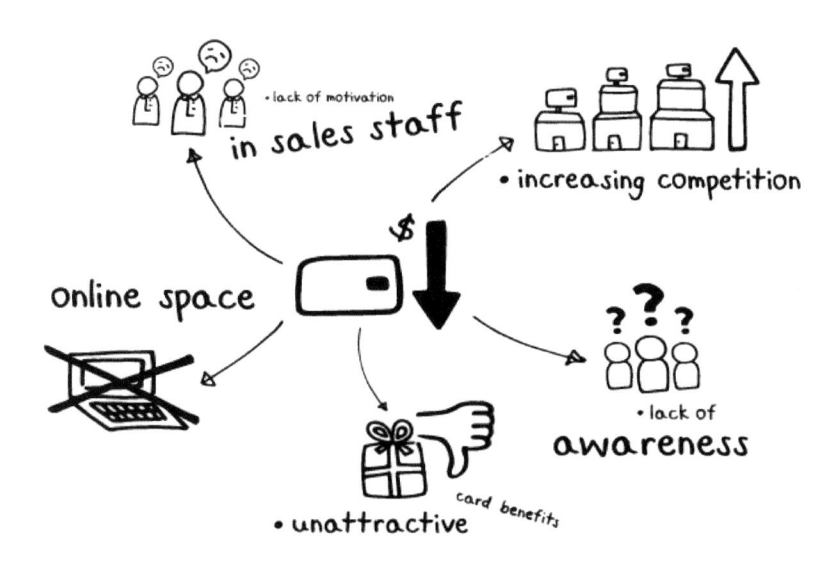

Learn how to draw your communication.

Lastly, it is important to draw your communication for the stakeholders to understand your concepts or ideas. Break your concept or idea into a persona and use simple questions to define it. Notice that the simple questions will help the audience to understand the central concept better.

Below is the example of typical product concept which you should draw:

Learn how to draw your communication.

List of user-centered benefits which define the product concept:

WHAT ARE MY BENEFITS?

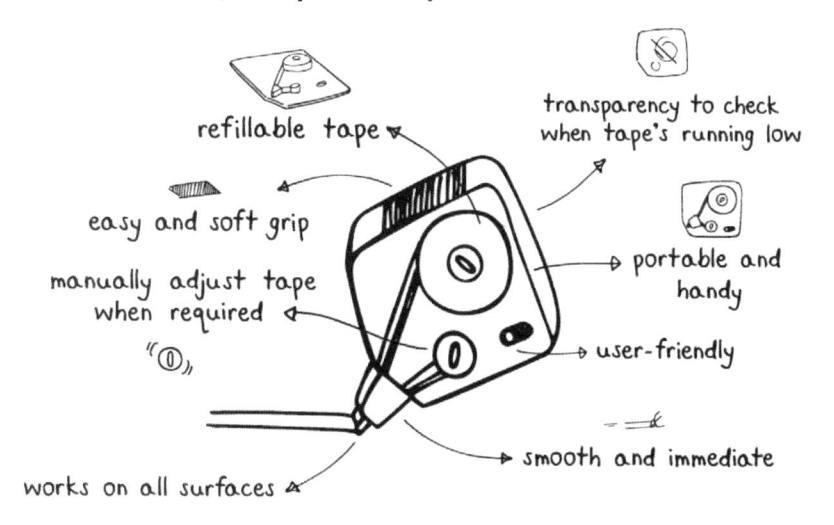

- refillable tape
- transparency to check when tape's running low
- easy and soft grip
- manually adjust tape when required
- portable and handy
- user-friendly
- smooth and immediate
- works on all surfaces

Define the context that the product concept could be used:

WHO DO I WORK WITH?

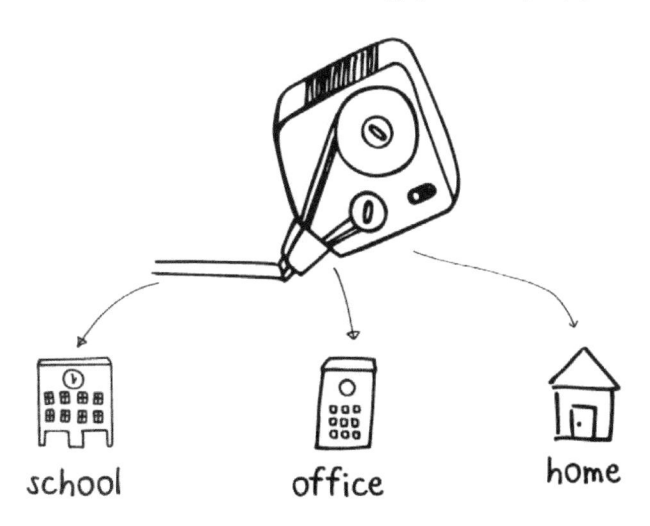

- school
- office
- home

135

HOW TO START FACILITATION BY DRAWING?

Drawing is a great tool to get people's creative juices flowing, and stimulate problem solving skills, but what do we do when we hit an impasse? How do we prevent ourselves from getting bogged down in details, and arguing in circles?

This is why a good facilitator is so important. So, what makes a good facilitator?

Understand the role of the facilitator

Remain neutral and stay objective. Your role is to draw the processes and conditions that enable a group to discuss, plan and decide. Conduct the discussion without trying to direct the group to a particular outcome.

Provide structure to the discussion

- Decide on the structure of the meeting, either independently or with your client.
- Build rapport (with some form of ice-breaker), and assure stakeholders that your objective is to help them. This helps the stakeholder to feel comfortable of your role as a facilitator and immediately to address the issues at hand.
- Ask questions *(See Ask the Right Questions)* to stakeholders to define the project.

Record the discussion by drawing for all to see

Visualize all points discuss on the board. We can draw the problems *(Using Draw the Problem activity)* or you can draw processes *(Using Draw your Journey activity)*. Otherwise you can draw outcomes and opportunities *(Using Draw a Poster activity)*.
The main objective is to make sure everyone is aligned with your drawings.

Ensure productive group behaviors

- Always refer to agreements when necessary to get the group back on track.
- Include everyone. Be sure all members have an opportunity to be heard
- Look for common ground.
- Deal with conflict by talking about the facts.

Summarize results

Summarize key points at the end of the session for:
- Learning
- Action points

CHAPTER 6 — BELIEVE YOU CAN DRAW

SUMMARY POINTS

You need to cultivate the belief that you can draw.

You need to communicate by drawing because you can agree better visually and it saves you time.

You need to create your own visual library.

You need to understand how to draw a journey, a problem and communicate your idea as part of your skill set.

You can facilitate meetings by drawing in 5 simple steps.

"IF YOU CAN DREAM IT, YOU CAN DO IT."

-WALT DISNEY, CREATOR AND ENTREPRENEUR

CHAPTER 7

COMMIT TO IDEATE

CHAPTER 7
COMMIT TO IDEATE

To paraphrase an old quote – "ideate is the art of the possible."

Ideation is the creative process of generating, developing and communicating new ideas, where an idea is understood as a basic element of thought expressed in words, visuals or form.

The goal of this commitment is not hundreds of ideas; it's one big idea.

Hence, every design thinker's mindset is to never stop at one idea - the more ideas we have, the greater our chances are that one of them will be a good solution to the problem.

The ideate phase is that magical place where:

The team's collective experiences and talents come together.
An image, or a word, will act as a catalyst for an idea.
From ideas, innovative solutions will spring forth.

Don't close your mind off to anything. This is design thinking at its most exhilarating! You need to cultivate your heart and commit to ideate.

In this chapter, you will learn:
Why do we need to ideate?
What are rules of ideation?
How to facilitate an ideation session?
How to build a creative culture?
What are the tools of ideation?
How to converge your ideas?

WHY DO YOU NEED TO IDEATE?

I feel that this quote best captures why we need to ideate:-
It's not about coming up with the 'right' idea, it's about generating the broadest range of possibilities."
– Hasso Plattner, Institute of Design at Stanford

As such, we should:

Explore more options
The more ideas you have, the greater your chance to identify a good solution to a problem.

Be more ready to make good decisions
You will be more ready to make decisions once you have explored all the options. This is the same analogy of the clothes buying process- you will be more sure of your purchase when you shopped at different stores and tried different fittings.

Build on ideas from diverse experience
Two heads are better than one. Creating ideas in a team is dynamic and Usually, very good ideas will develop.

WHAT ARE RULES OF IDEATION?

We have identified the question or problem. Now, in the ideate phase, we have to find the solution. To ideate means to think critically, and examine the problem from different perspectives. There is usually more than one solution to a problem. The real question is, "What is the best solution?"

This is the opposite of traditional linear thinking, which acts like an intellectual straight jacket at times.

Welcome and respect any ideas from anybody

Encourage wild ideas and out of the box thinking

Defer judgement- there are no wrong ideas

Facilitate one conversation at a time

Be visual and make quick prototypes

Encourage building on ideas

Focus on quantity not quality

CHAPTER 7   COMMIT TO IDEATE

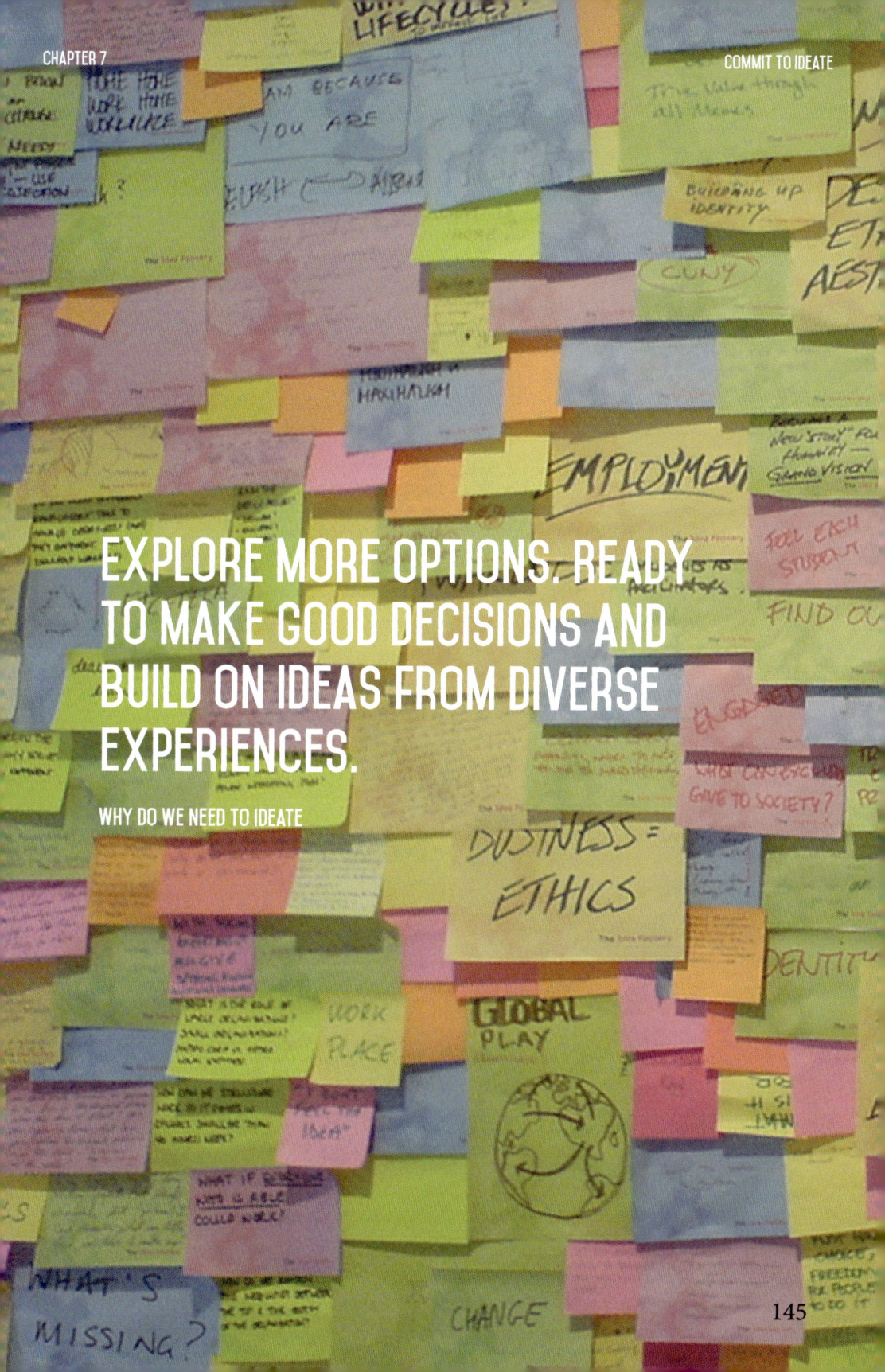

EXPLORE MORE OPTIONS. READY TO MAKE GOOD DECISIONS AND BUILD ON IDEAS FROM DIVERSE EXPERIENCES.

WHY DO WE NEED TO IDEATE

HOW TO FACILITATE AN IDEATION SESSION?

One of a design thinker's roles is to facilitate an ideation session with his stakeholders. Below are few essential steps throughout the facilitation that you may want to follow. Do not worry if you feel uncomfortable or unsure, it comes with experience!

Manage a creative space

Create a space which encourages co-creation and collaboration, and most importantly, without any notion of hierarchy. For example, no board-room type of meeting space where the "head" sits right at the end.

Be ready with necessary design tools using the *TOOLS and RESOURCES checklist*.

Set expectation

Brief your stakeholders about the ideation session- let them know the *Rules of Ideation (above)*. Walk them through your process so that your stakeholders are mentally prepared.

Define the problem

Define the problem statement *(Refer to PROBLEM STATEMENT template)* and have the design brief ready *(refer to DESIGN BRIEF)*.

Conduct ideation

Refer to the *5 Common Ideation Techniques* later in the chapter.

Sort the ideas

Sort or group the ideas. *(See 3 Simple Ways to Converge)*

Evaluate and create action steps

Define some action steps ahead for the next meeting.

CHAPTER 7　　　　　　　　　　　　　　　　　　　　　　　　　　COMMIT TO IDEATE

1. MANAGE A CREATIVE SPACE
2. SET EXPECTATION
3. DEFINE THE PROBLEM
4. CONDUCT IDEATION
5. SORT THE IDEAS
6. EVALUATE AND CREATE ACTION STEPS

HOW DO WE FACILITATE AN IDEATION SESSION

147

HOW TO BUILD A CREATIVE CULTURE?

A creative culture is one where people feel comfortable in expressing their ideas in the workplace. It is a way of work and should be encouraged from the top management down.

You are in a creative culture when:
- You are appreciated for what you do and who you are.
- You feel appreciated when you suggest new ideas.
- You are given the freedom to do your work in your own way.
- You feel comfortable collaborating and co-creating with anyone (top bosses included).
- You are encouraged to experiment.
- Your boss spends time to explain the reasons and politics behind projects.
- You are not restricted by chain-of-commands through your bosses.
- Someone will listen to your ideas.
- Generation of good ideas are rewarded.

3 WAYS TO UNLEASH CREATIVITY IN THE WORKPLACE

Reward creativity
If you want to get employees to think out-of-the-box and provide good ideas and solutions, you need to motivate them with some form of rewards. Rewards could be tangible like monetary incentives or even intangible such as recognition from bosses.

Good ideas have to be taken seriously and to be implemented- otherwise employees will be demotivated to suggest good ideas that will not be implemented.

Creative working space
Implement a designated space where brainstorming and ideation sessions should take place- a collaborative environment with necessary design tools and resources to support creativity. Ensure there are plenty of whiteboards or flipcharts to visualize ideas and concepts- even as a showcase to inspire others to work in the same manner.

Encourage collaboration and co-creation
Discourage employees from working by themselves and encourage them to work in multi-disciplinary teams from different departments to create ideas and solve problems. Create an open friendly atmosphere where everyone is approachable for discussion with transparency and passion to help each other.

DIVERGENT- 5 COMMON IDEATION TECHNIQUES

The purpose of ideation is to create choices. The divergent and Explorative thinking cap has to be on in order to create as many solutions to a problem as possible.

Ideation has two types of use. First, ideation allows for initial exploration, where the team do not have any initial ideas to start. Second, ideation also allows for pushing of boundaries where we increase our frame of thought to more than just a few ideas at hand.

One common thing for ideation is that you need a group (two or more) in order to brainstorm effectively. That also means that the commitment to ideate must naturally come from the team, and not just depend on one creative individual to deliver the ideas.

There are 5 common brainstorming techniques as follows:

Initial Exploration
Brainwriting
Problem Brainstorming (Nyaka)
Sharing Brainstorming (NHK Method)

Pushing Boundaries
SCAMPER
What if?

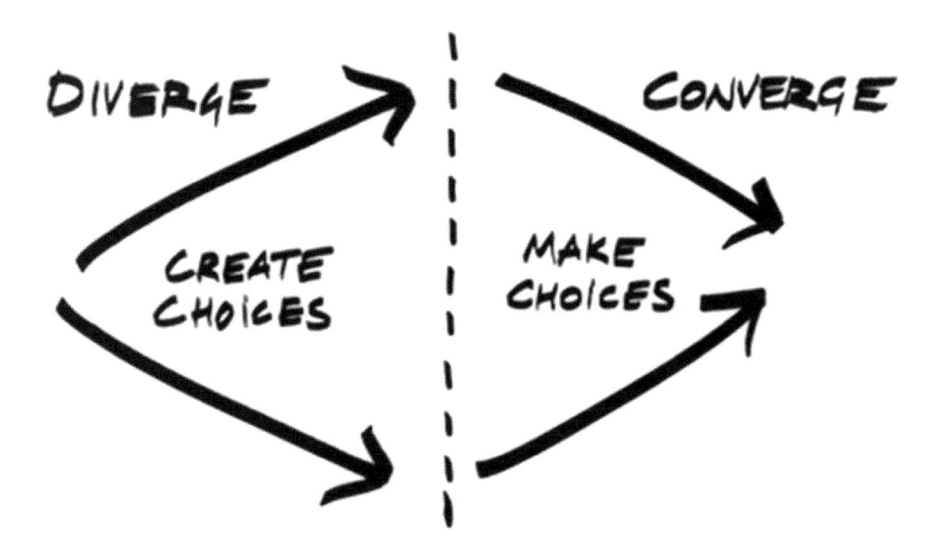

1. INITIAL EXPLORATION - BRAINWRITING

What is it?:
Brainwriting is a powerful method in leveraging the building of ideas in a systematic manner.

How to deliver?:
1. Define the problem
2. Each person should brainstorm three ideas in two minutes on a piece of paper.
3. Then have them pass the sheet of paper to the person on the left.
4. Have the next person to build upon or add to the existing ideas by writing/ drawing their own ideas underneath the existing ideas. Allow 3 minutes.
5. Repeat the process around the table with the next person building on existing ideas or add on new ideas, until the paper comes back to the originator.
6. Share all the ideas on the table and pick out a couple of outstanding ones.

Resources:
Pens
Post-its
Paper
Table
White board / Wall
Refreshments

2. INITIAL EXPLORATION
- PROCESS PROBLEM BRAINSTORMING (NYAKA)

What is it?:

Nyaka brainstorming is a method that emphasize on exploring problems and solutions to problems. It is usually done with a customer journey or a work process that has a breakdown in different multiple problems with the experience.

It subsequently allows to understand which is the wicked problem and subsequently prioritize a hierarchy of ideas.

How to deliver?:

1. Team to build a customer journey or a work process that they want to identify the problems or issues.
2. Facilitator asks the group to define as many things that are wrong with the design of the process / service / experience and write them on the left space of a line.
3. Facilitator asks the group to define solutions for as many of the problems defined as possible and write them on the right space of the line.
4. Create a hierarchy of problems and hierarchy of solutions for each problem.
5. Based on the discussion, the group can decide which solutions to further develop based on certain criterias, and make prototypes.

Resources:

Pens
Post-its
Paper
Table
White board / Wall
Refreshments

3. INITIAL EXPLORATION - SHARING BRAINSTORMING (NHK METHOD)

What is it?:
The NHK brainstorming method allows members to build ideas through the sharing of ideas from another member.

How to deliver?:
1. Define the problem
2. Each participant writes down five ideas on five separate cards.
3. In groups of 5, while each person shares one idea from his card, the others will create an idea out of his idea.
4. The sequence continues around the table until there are many ideas on the table.
5. Collect and group the ideas into more meaningful categories.
6. Select a couple of outstanding ideas to prototype and test.

Resources:
Pens
Post-its
Paper
Table
Refreshments

4. PUSHING BOUNDARIES - SCAMPER

What is it?:

SCAMPER is a brainstorming technique and innovation method that uses seven words as prompts:
1. **Substitute**
2. **Combine**
3. **Adapt**
4. **Modify**
5. **Put to another Use**
6. **Eliminate**
7. **Reverse**

How to deliver?:

1. Select an idea / concept / existing product to apply the SCAMPER method
2. Facilitator will lead the team to ideate out of the box by asking questions based on SCAMPER
3. Create as many ideas based on the questions.
4. Analyse and prioritise
5. Select a couple of ideas to further develop and prototype.

Resources:

Pens
Post-its
Paper
Table
Flipchart / White board
Refreshments

4. PUSHING BOUNDARIES - SCAMPER

1. Substitute:
- What materials or elements could you substitute or swap to improve the product?
- What other product or process could you use?

2. Combine:
- What would happen if you combined this product with another, to create something new?
- How to combine purposes or objectives?

3. Adapt:
- What other context could you put your product into?
- What other products or ideas could you use for inspiration?

4. Modify:
- How could you change the shape, look, or feel of your product?
- What could you emphasize or highlight to create more value?

5. Put to Another Use
- Can you use this product some where else, perhaps in another industry?
- Who else could use this product?

6. Eliminate:
- How could you streamline or simplify this product?
- What would happen if you took away part of this product?

7. Reverse:
- How could you reorganize this product?
- What if you try to do the exact opposite of what you're trying to do now?

5. PUSHING BOUNDARIES - WHAT IF?

What is it?:
What if? is a brainstorming technique that push the boundaries of constraints or limitations over a concept / existing product. It follows the principle in asking new questions if you want new answers.

How to deliver?:
1. Select an idea / concept / existing product to apply the What if? method
2. Facilitator will lead the team to ideate out of the box by asking questions based on What if? The rest will chip in with more "what if" questions.
3. Create as many ideas based on the questions.
4. Analyse and prioritise
5. Select a couple of ideas to further develop and prototype.

Resources:
Pens
Post-its
Paper
Table
Flipchart / White board
Refreshments

What If Questions:

1. Scarcity / Abundance:
What if a car can run without petrol?

What if you have unlimited budget to change this website?

2. Extreme Simplicity:
What if the army fight with no soldiers?

What if you can apply for a bank loan in one step?

3. Opposite:
What if your mobile phone runs to you instead of you running to your mobile phone?

What if an employee pays the company to work instead of the company paying the employee?

CHAPTER 7 COMMIT TO IDEATE

DIVERGENT THINKING CREATE CHOICES WHILE CONVERGENT THINKING MAKE CHOICES.

CONCEPT OF IDEATION

CONVERGENT- 3 SIMPLE WAYS TO CONVERGE

After putting on the divergent thinking cap using various ideation techniques, you may have a lot of ideas on your plate. The key to moving forward with good and informed solutions is to know how to converge.

From having a lot of ideas, you now have to narrow down to one. Remember, the key objective of ideation is that ONE good idea or solution. Below are some frameworks that allow you to prioritize, organize and evaluate.

3 ways to converge your ideas:

1. Affinity Map
2. Prioritization Map
3. Idea Evaluation

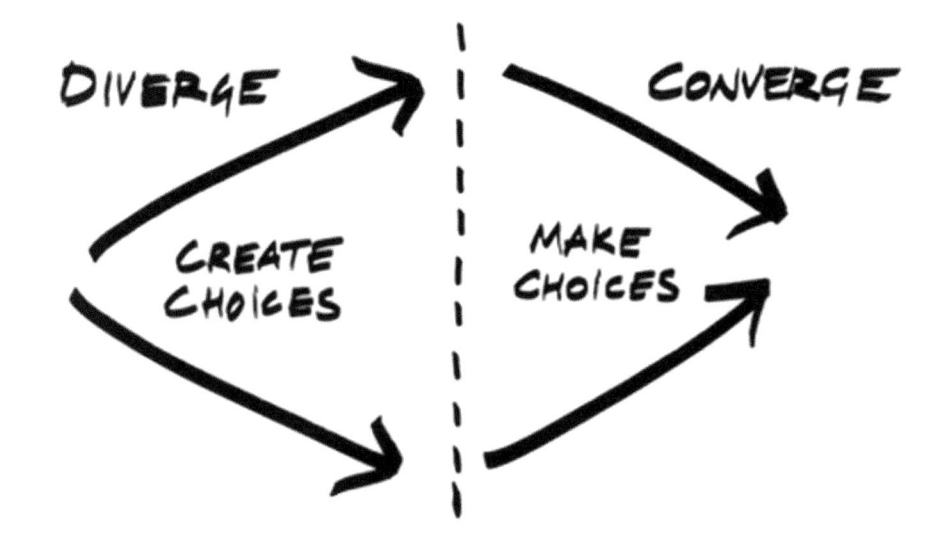

1. PRIORITISATION MAP

What is it?:

A prioritisation map allows you to map your ideas based on the ease of implementation against level of benefit to users. This allows you to make informed decision which ideas to start working on and which ideas to park for future implementation.

How to deliver?:

1. Map all your ideas onto the prioritisation map.
2. Decide which ideas would be good to proceed with- usually ideas that are easy to implement and of high benefit value should be done first.
3. Decide which other ideas that you intend to implement. Ideas of high benefit value but difficult to implement should be kept in view for future roadmap while you may want to discard some ideas that has low benefit value.

Resources:

Pens
Post-its
Paper
Table
Refreshments

EXAMPLE OF PRIORITISATION MAP

Improve Restaurant's Customer Experience

High Benefit

Park it later

More comfy seats

Ipad ordering system

Service training for all staff

New payment system

Do it now!

Easy to Implement

Difficult to Implement

Drones serving food

New sound system

CRM system

Discard

Low Benefit

2. AFFINITY MAP

What is it?:
An affinity map is a method that allows you to analyze and organize your ideas by discovering relationships to develop a design direction based on affinities among your ideas. This could be done within the team to agree on the ideas in logical categories.

How to deliver?:
1. Map all your ideas onto the affinity map.
2. Decide which ideas have affinity with each other and group them together and create a name for these group of ideas.
3. Do the same for all the ideas until you find that there are 3 or 4 very strong affinity groups of ideas. Discard the rest of the ideas that you think don't belong.
4. You may decide with your team which design direction could be the way to proceed.

Resources:
Pens
Post-its
Paper
Table
Refreshments

EXAMPLE OF AFFINITY MAP

Ideas to Facilitate Classroom Learning

Random Post-its of ideas

Categorise and group the ideas

3. IDEA EVALUATION

What is it?:
Idea evaluation is a table of criteria to compare and understand the difference among your ideas based on the criterias. This could be done if you want to evaluate and select the ideas together with the stakeholders.

How to deliver?:
1. Map all your ideas onto the idea evaluation table.
2. Write down key points of each idea based on each criteria.
3. Evaluate and decide which ideas to go ahead by eliminating ideas which do not fulfill important criterias.

Resources:
Pens
Post-its
Paper
Table
Refreshments

EXAMPLE OF **IDEA EVALUATION**

How to Evaluate 4 Ideas Based on Customer Impact

Evaluation Criteria	Idea A	Idea B	Idea C	Idea D
Customer Impact	++ Greatly benefits the customers	− May not	+ Value for the young	+ Will benefit in the future
Business Impact				
Potential Improvement				
Feasibility				
Innovativeness				
XYZ				

SUMMARY POINTS

You need to cultivate your heart and commit to ideate.

You need to ideate in order to explore more options, make good decisions and build on ideas from diverse experience.

There are 6 steps to facilitate an ideation session.

You need both divergent and convergent thinking in order to create choices and then make choices.

There are 5 ways to ideate for initial exploration and pushing boundaries while there are 3 ways to organise and select your ideas.

"I HAVE NOT FAILED. I'VE JUST FOUND 10,000 WAYS THAT WON'T WORK."

–THOMAS EDISON, INVENTOR

CHAPTER 8
PROTOTYPE TO TEST

CHAPTER 8
PROTOTYPE TO TEST

You always need to prototype to test.

Prototyping gives you the opportunity to demonstrate your idea or solution to stakeholders / end-users visually so that they have a better understanding- so that you can get feedback and refine the solution.

One of the classic examples is the Microsoft Zune mp3 player, and its sequel Zune HD. Launched in 2006, Zune was Microsoft's answer to Apple's i Pod. Unfortunately, it had a mixed reception. Some praised its features, while other reviewers criticized its design and bulkiness.

In 2009, thousands of Zune players froze Microsoft said it was due to software problems with its internal clock). Zune was finally discontinued after 2010.

In my opinion, this was a classic case of a company pressured to launch its product/ service hastily and hoping for the best, without adequate prototyping or testing. The end-users got "burnt" and complained, and the design team had to do the painful, expensive and demanding task of reworking and redesigning.

One of the key skills of the design thinker is to ensure that we prototype and test every solution early and cheaply- so as to discover any problems or issues before the product is rolled out.

It saves cost and effort throughout the process and minimizes chances for errors.

In this chapter, you will learn:
Why do we need to prototype?
What could be a prototype?
How to make a prototype?
What is a test?
How do we conduct a test- experience lab?

WHAT YOU COULD USE AS A PROTOTYPE?

A prototype is an early-stage model or visual of a product/service built to be tested or as a thing to be learned from or refined.

You can use absolutely anything to build it. From rough cardboard models, paper, wireframes or simple concept sketches to refined factory-made products or pre-launched apps.

Ideally, it is recommended that a prototype should be cheap, fast and easy- so as to eliminate the pain of cost and effort- should refinement and iteration be needed.

Types of rough prototypes:
- Physical mockup in cardboards / paper
- Sketches
- Wireframes
- Storyboard or script
- Role-plays or experiential display

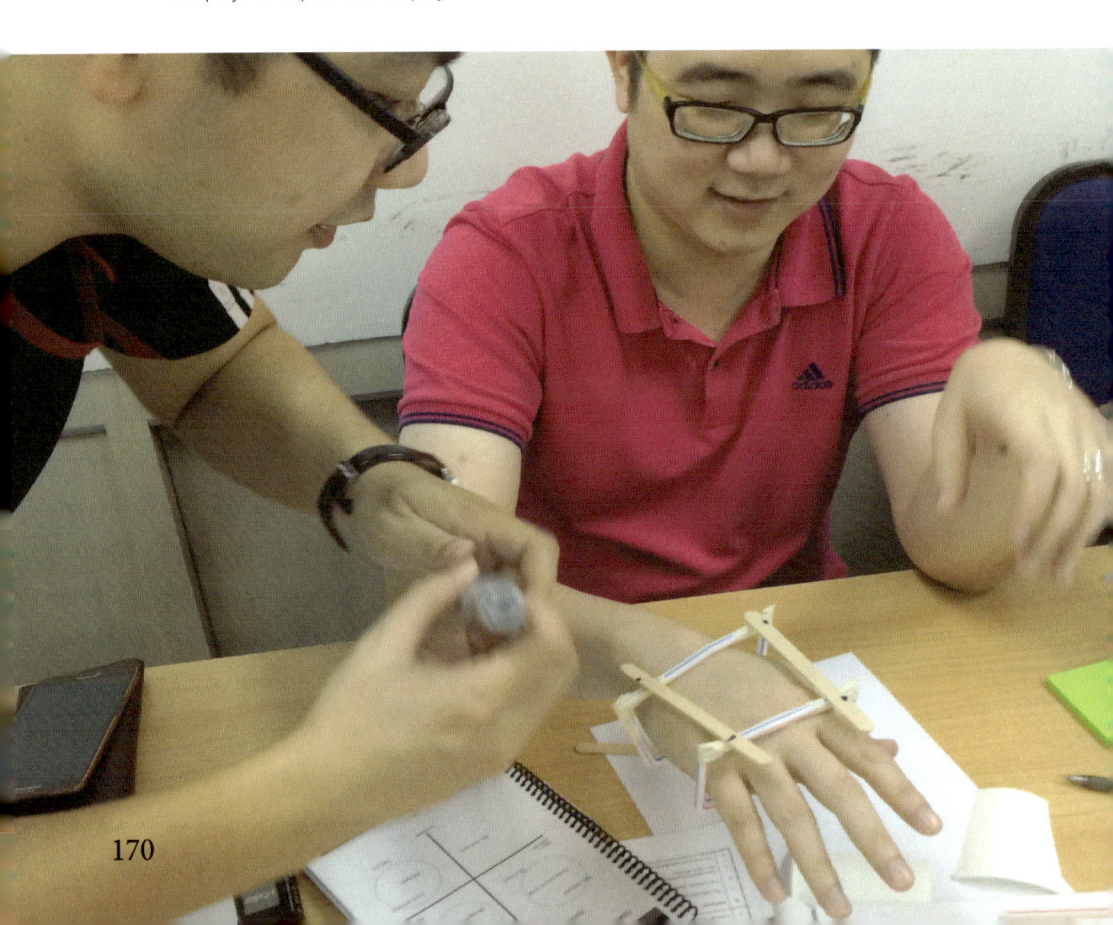

WHY DO WE NEED A PROTOTYPE?

The main benefit of prototyping to find out something that you don't already know. You can go through a very productive brainstorming session or do a very detailed write-up about a particular product/gadget, but there are always some things that you will miss.

For example, can an end-user easily figure out a new feature on your gadget? Is it easy to find? Is it easy to use? These are all questions that can't be easily answered in powerpoint presentations and concept papers.

A more finished prototype is also good to show to your bosses and financiers.

- Find design issues early

- Iterate more quickly on a design concept

- Compare design variations quickly

- Gather design feedback better

- Good presentational tool

- Encourage collaboration

- Cheap, fast and easy

- Gather design feedback better

WHY DO WE TEST?

A test is an assessment to establish the validity, reliability and quality of design of a product or service. You can conduct tests in any form of formality as long as you are able to achieve your end objective. For example, a test could just be as simple as walking up to your neighbour with a prototype and asking a few questions. Otherwise, a test could be conducted in a more structured manner.

We test our prototypes because:

So we can validate and iterate quickly

Match expectations of end users

Evaluate feedback

To communicate results to end users

HOW TO CONDUCT A STRUCTURED TEST - EXPERIENCE LAB?

An experience lab is a structured session where you get to talk, listen, observe and find out about the customers' attitude, behavior and opinion towards products and services. The objectives are to get insight - such as understanding "how's" and "why's" of customers.

Customers are usually requested to do specific user tasks on channels from mobile, web, paper (such as brochures, or forms) or physical objects, and give their comments at the end of their tasks. The facilitator (you) will usually sit beside the customer to observe, ask questions and listen. Separately, a group of other observers will observe, listen and take notes.

Who needs to attend?

1. Participants
Usually sampling size of participants is about 6-8 customers. Selecting the profile of customers is determined based on project needs and requirements. Recruitment should usually be made 2 weeks before the experience lab sessions and you may need to prepare incentives in exchange of their precious feedback and time.

2. Stakeholders
All stakeholders involved in the design thinking process should attend as observers. They are required to take down notes during the lab sessions and participate actively during the debrief session.

3. Vendors
Sometimes it might be useful to invite vendors (people in charge of fabricating your prototypes) to also attend your sessions so that the discussions after that will be more aligned with common objectives and tackle common issues together.

How to go about through the process?

Generally, there are 5 phases of the process to take note, although it could be tasked by different team members to deal with each phase.

1. Define project goals and user profile
2. Recruit users
3. Conduct experience labs
4. Analyze and recommend
5. Present findings

CHAPTER 8 | PROTOTYPE TO TEST

1. DEFINE PROJECT GOALS & USER PROFILE
2. RECRUIT USERS
3. CONDUCT EXPERIENCE LABS
4. ANALYZE AND RECOMMEND
5. PRESENT FINDINGS

5 STEPS OF EXPERIENCE LABS

5 STEPS OF EXPERIENCE LABS

The experience lab is where the rubber meets the road, as the Americans like to say. You've got a beta version prototype ready and you are going to test it out with a third party user.

This is where to find out how well your idea and solution works. Don't be afraid if things don't go as well as you expect, or if it totally fails! If it fails, we go back to the drawing board. Besides, we learn far more from our failures than our successes!

Define project goals and user profile

Make use of what you have learned *(Chapter 5 - Ask the Right Questions)* to define your goals for the project and understand what the stakeholders want. Create some form of user persona *(Chapter 4 - Think Users First)* to understand who is your target audience.

Recruit users

Usually for experience labs, we recruit only 6-8 users. Studies have shown that with 6-8 users, we are able to uncover approximately 80% of the issues with a given product. Also understand the diversity of your target audience. If you are designing a new trading platform, you should understand the different segments - savvy investors, newbies to trading, as well as mid-level users.

During recruitment, be sure to tell them the venue, date and time for the users to be there. Offer some form of incentive as a reward for their participation.

Conduct experience labs

On the actual day, you may be talking to 3-4 users at 1.5 hours block each

Generally, each session can be divided in 4 parts:
- Brief and Interview user (10 mins)
- Prototype / User Test walk through (40mins)
- Wrap up with user (10mins)
- Debrief with observers (30mins)

Analyze and recommend

Have a final debrief with the stakeholders / observers to analyze the findings and recommend some changes to the design of the prototype.

What are the plusses? What are the minuses? What are the additional ideas that were gleaned from the labs?

Present the findings

Finalize your findings to a deck so that you can present to others what your team has found in the labs.

HOW TO CONDUCT THE INTERVIEW?

The interview is actually a very critical phase – this is where you get valuable data! It is very common for the test user to be very nervous at this stage. So it is important to make him/her feel at ease. That way, he/she will be more honest, and more forthcoming with you! Otherwise, the user will clam up, and be afraid to say anything, for fear of offending you, and you won't learn what you need to know.

Brief the user

Right from the beginning, when you meet up with the customer, greet him/her a warm welcome. You may find this checklist helpful.

1. Welcome participant and introduce myself.
2. Introduce the project brief
3. Explain the overall structure of the presentation (eg "This interview will take about 1 hour, where I will have a brief chit-chat session, followed by using prototype and leave the last 10 min to summarise)
4. "Feel free to speak your mind, voice your views along the way"
5. "Tell us what you think, whether it is positive or negative"
6. "This is not a test of you in any way, but rather it is the test of the project"
7. "Do stop me if you have any questions or if you are uncomfortable at any point of time"
8. "The whole interview will be viewed from another room, where my colleagues will be gathering insights from our interview and writing down notes, so that I can concentrate on my interview with you"
9. "Interview will not be recorded"
10. Confidentiality of participant "Your name and particulars will be kept confidential"
11. Manage expectation of prototype "This prototype may not be a final piece, so expect something that work or something that does not."

1

2

3

HOW TO CONDUCT THE INTERVIEW?

Conduct interview and user-testing

Ask some basic questions to find out more about the customer and his/her opinion about the topic. For example if you want to know about a credit card customer:

Tell me more about yourself?
What do you think about having credit cards?
What credit cards do you have? What do you use them for?
What do you think about OUR credit cards?

Show the prototype and give instructions for specific tasks that the customer have to do. Observe and ask probing questions if need be.

Scenario	Probing Questions
When you observed something	**I have observed that...** do you have any comments on that?
When user asks for a solution	What do you think? **(Don't give any solutions)**
When user is stalling	What are you **thinking** right now?
When user is expecting an outcome	What would you **expect**? Do you **expect** anything? Is this what you have **expected**?
When user is pondering next action	What would you do next? (**Next course of action**)
When you want to know the reason	**Why? Why? Why?**
When user express a feeling	How do **feel** this way?
When you want to know a process	How will you use? **(Understand the process)**
When you want to know immediate reaction	What is your impression?
When you discuss the future	What do you think will happen next? **(Discussing the future)**
When you discuss in retrospect	How was it? What has happened? **(Retrospective)**

Summarize and wrap up

Allow customer to provide final reflections of the prototype or review any other points that were left out during the user test. Be ready to paraphrase the feedback that was mentioned during the test and wait for agreement.

HOW TO CONDUCT THE OBSERVER'S DEBRIEF?

Make sure you remember to debrief the observers as well as the user. The observers have to be very impartial and objective. If they start talking and discussing things, they will subconsciously affect each other's findings.

Therefore, it is important to remember this:

Ensure all observers follow rules while you conduct interviews

What you can't do:
- Talk aloud
- Influence other observers with opinions
- Think about solutions now
- Justify yourself or the project
- Start discussion before the interview is over

What you can do:
- Be objective, curious and open
- Listen carefully
- Capture verbal and non-verbal cues
- Write down all problems / opportunities
- Stop guessing and start knowing

Ensure all observers receive a template to write things down during interview

Refer to the *OBSERVER template* on the next page.

Facilitate the observers after the interview

Bring out a large flipchart and talk things through with the observers. Seek agreement with all observers and write it down so that everyone is aligned.

Park opinions and opportunities to a separate space so that you can revisit them at a later stage.

After all the sessions are over, have final debrief with the observers and stakeholders to analyze the findings and recommend some changes that will improve the project.

EXAMPLE OF **OBSERVER TEMPLATE**

Observer's note on feedback of Phone A

Customer profile / background

> Johnathan Lim, 38
> Lawyer, single

Pros of concept / prototype

> Could turn on Phone A easily
>
> Attracted by the colours
>
> Commented on the ease of the buttons
>
> Pleased with the features included in Phone A

Cons of concept / prototype

> Confused by the user interface for settings
>
> Frowned at the price of Phone A
>
> Commented that the size of Phone A is too big for his pocket

Any other feedback

> Asked if there is any problem if he is to switch to Phone A from his existing phone.

EXAMPLE OF PROTOTYPE EVALUATION

Evaluation Criteria	Prototype A	Prototype B	Prototype C	Prototype D
Functionality		Achieved product objectives		
Cost			Too expensive for all users	
Aesthetics		Jane is attracted by the colours		
Usability	All users think it is simple		Simple to understand	
Maintenance				Peter feels this is not durable
XYZ				

SUMMARY POINTS

You need to cultivate your hands to prototype to test.

You can use any form of materials that you can use your hands to build or visualise to create a prototype.

You understand the reasons why you need to prototype or test.

There are 5 phases of conducting an experience lab.

You understand there are skills and methods required to conduct the interview as well as facilitating the observers.

END
BY DANIEL LING

"Insanity is doing the same things over and over again and expecting a different result."
- Albert Einstein

At this point of writing, I am already close to publishing and distributing this book throughout Singapore, Southeast Asia, Hong Kong, Taiwan and the rest of the world. I feel an important burden to uphold by sharing my experience in design thinking as well as the action plan and mindsets that comes with it.

By sharing this knowledge written in this book, I implore two things from you and with that I have fulfilled a life objective.

1. Apply what you have learnt

Start small but start. Wisdom from a quote, inspiration from an activity or a practical tool from a template- all these are little building blocks to apply to your individual life, workplace, school or society. Be constantly mindful of the things that you have learnt and apply design thinking everywhere you go.

2. Be the change agent

Be the salt of the earth and light of the world. Einstein implied that change is inevitable and only a fool will not embrace change. Notice that once you start the change to be a design thinker and solve
problems in a unique manner, people will see and people will follow- especially when you deliver the right results.

For design thinking training workshops, talks or consultation with expert design thinker Daniel Ling, contact emerge.creatives@gmail.com to discuss opportunities.